ALA Studies in Librarianship
No. 7

D0783061

Getting Books to Children

An Exploration of Publisher–Market Relations

JOSEPH TUROW

AMERICAN LIBRARY ASSOCIATION
Chicago 1978

Library of Congress Cataloging in Publication Data

Turow, Joseph.
    Getting books to children.

    (ALA studies in librarianship ; no. 7)
    Based on the author's thesis, University of Pennsylvania.
    Bibliography: p.
    1.   Children's literature—Publishing. 2. Libraries
and publishing. 3. Booksellers and bookselling.
I. Title. II. Series: American Library Association.
ALA studies in librarianship ; no. 7.
Z286.C48T87   658.8'09'070573   78–24103
ISBN 0–8389–0276–6

Printed in the United States of America

Contents

Preface

This study is about the production and distribution of books to children. Despite the enormous amount of material currently available on children's literature, some basic questions about the books our youngsters read have been virtually ignored. What activities are carried out by publishing firms in their choosing, producing, and marketing of children's books? What general and specific guidelines direct their activities? Why are the titles—and the publishing imprints—found in school and public libraries often so different from the ones found in bookstores and department stores? How do the interactions between librarians and editors, between publishers' representatives and bookstore agents, influence the types of books produced and the titles that end up on library and bookstore shelves?

The answers to these basic questions are not simple. Children's book publishing, like every other organized process of symbol production, takes place through a complex web of organizational and interpersonal relationships. Only an in-depth, critical analysis of these relationships and illuminate the process. This study is a descriptive one, and groups are not singled out as heroes or villains. Instead, the purpose is to provide a systematic investigation of forces guiding the production and distribution of children's books to libraries (the library market) and to commercial outlets (the mass market). The concern with literary values found among the librarians and library market publishing personnel I studied should be noted, however. The last chapter of this work explores possibilities for exporting this eager creativity to other markets that serve children, including the mass market.

When I began this study, I did not fully comprehend the magnitude of the activity I was undertaking. The intimidating immensity of that job was fortunately masked by the assistance of many individuals during the course of the research and writing. Because space does not permit naming them all, and because the generous people in the organizations concerned prefer to remain anonymous, a general expression of deep gratitude must suffice. Certain individuals must be publicly thanked, however, as without their assistance I would never have accomplished this task. Esther Hautzig, a cherished relative and award-winning children's book writer, was the original reason for my interest in the children's book industry and has been unstintingly generous in her help. Moral and intellectual support has also been forthcoming from my friends at the Annenberg School of Communications and the Graduate School of Education, University of Pennsylvania. Warm thanks are due my editor, Herbert Bloom, and professors George Gerbner, Neal Gross, Larry Gross, and William Melody, who guided my doctoral studies.

The concern and help of my family have been the greatest encouragement of all. Sol, Masha, Jerry, Mark, and Debbie Gabry—my uncle, aunt, and cousins—have always been interested. My brother, Victor, has been helpful with good ideas and good conversation. Abraham and Danuta Turow have played a profound role in the development, execution, and completion of this study. In many ways, they have been my collaborators. To them, my parents, I have dedicated this work.

Introduction

Mass communication perspectives curiously have not been applied to the juvenile book industry, an industry that periodically percolates controversies in its trade press, ones that boil over onto general circulation magazines and newspapers. The reason for this absence is clarified by the fact that research on the production and distribution of children's books from any perspective is not very extensive. Most studies have tended to focus only on the selection guidelines of librarians or editors and, in doing so, concentrated on particular policies regarding a special aspect of the selection process, that of censorship. Little systematic attention had been paid to the myriad organizational factors that cause people in organizations connected with books—publishing firms, libraries, and commercial distribution outlets—to hold certain guidelines and to choose for publication and purchase certain books over others. Most of the research has been conducted from library schools, and little cross-fertilization of ideas between scholars of library science and those of mass media organizations has taken place. The latter, for their part, have been content to claim the electronic media, films, and newspapers as their research realms and tended to ignore book publishing.

Actually, however, children's book publishing is a fruitful area in which to explore certain ideas relating to mass communication. The reasons for this are rooted in the scale of the industry's firms. One of the hallmarks of mass communication is that it is carried out by organizations interacting with other organizations in the process of producing and distributing content. The organizational nature of mass communication thus has an important influence on the shaping of the content ordinarily released to large, dispersed audiences. Popular images of vast Hollywood film and television studios—and publishing empires—illustrate on the simplest level the distance between this type of communication and more traditional forms. This difference is not without consequence for the artist, the creator of the message. When dealing with the mass media, the artist is much further removed from the end-product of his or her work than if it was created and distributed through nonorganizational channels. The distancing of the artist from the work is accompanied by a diminishing of power over his or her own creative destiny: for the privilege of reaching more people than one individual could ever possibly reach through interpersonal communication, the artist must submit many important decisions—including the decision to display his or her talents—to organizational selectors whose first priority is the economic health of their firm.

It has taken almost two centuries for scholars to recognize that the industrialized production of messages is a revolutionary way of making ideas public. Consequently, little systematic research has been completed on the influence that this process has upon the messages that blanket modern society and comprise a good portion of its symbolic environment. Scholars are now recognizing the need to understand the organizations that produce mass media material, however, and this need also applies to mass media complexes—that is, to informal conglomerations of organizations continually interacting in the process of producing and distributing mass media content.

Many different kinds of organizations interact in the continual activity of producing and distributing mass media material. Suppliers, labor unions, government regulatory agencies—these and other entities deal with production firms and likely mark their output. However, the organizations that doubtless have the most influence among mass media production firms are those that subsidize the material producers release. Two types of organizations—investors and patrons—can often be distinguished in this regard. Investors put up money in advance of production and purchase. They include banks, large investment syndicates, private foundations, and government agencies. Their up-front money is often provided with the expectation that the producers will eventually find patrons for the mass media material created. For example, in the American television complex, banks and stockholders invest in particular production firms on the belief that enough advertisers, or patrons, will pay to be identified with the producers' shows to make their investment profitable. Similarly, in American book publishing, investors provide capital to publishers with the expectation that a profitable number of distribution outlets will purchase the books. For most trade publishers, these outlets are the patrons.

In essence, then, patrons are the customers of producers; the patrons decide by their purchases whether or not particular mass media material will be released to the public. It follows that the patrons' importance is involved in their being most directly responsible for the organizations' solvency. Since it would be unrealistic to deal in depth with all the multiorganizational interactions in a mass media complex during the course of one study, this investigation focuses on the critical interaction between production organizations and the organizations that purchase their goods. Gerbner has called this kind of interaction a "client relationship."[1]

A comparative study of client relationships in the children's book industry can be particularly useful to the mass communication researcher. As Lanes has noted, general children's nontext book publishing contains two separate segments with distinct, generally nonoverlapping production and distribution outlet organizations.[2] The library market segment consists mostly of nonprofit patron institutions, whose usually publicly employed selectors buy books from library-oriented publishing firms. The commercially oriented mass market for children's books is dominated by department, chain, and bookstore patrons that support a different group of publishing firms. But in both cases, the publisher is the producer, the outlet is the patron. And, in both sets of client relationship, the patron organizations function as ultimate distributors of producers' books to the children and/or their parents. It is perhaps important to stress that children and parents who buy or borrow children's books are not patrons or clients according to the terminology of this investigation; rather they are consumers or publics who must choose titles from the choices offered to them by stores and libraries.

The concern of this book, then, is to examine the manner in which the mass market and library market client relationships help shape choices of new books awaiting children and their parents in book and department stores, as compared to those awaiting them in public libraries. From a theoretical perspective, the work is concerned with the consequences that these different client relationships have on the process of producing and distributing content directed towards the same purported audience. In order to accomplish these goals, a comparative case study was conducted. One important production organization from each segment and one important patron, or distribution outlet, organization from the library market —two from the mass market—were studied with the goal of charting the influences upon the selectors of content within each organization and, extensionally, of gauging the influence of the client relationships on various aspects of book selection at both the production and distribution outlet levels. The patron organizations were chosen from the same city so that the consequences of different client relationships for the distribution of a sizable number of juvenile books within the same area could be examined.

The organizations described in this book have been given pseudonymns but they do, in fact, exist. The library market publishing and outlet organizations will be called R&A Publishing and Metrosystem, respectively. The mass market publisher will be called Global Publishing; the bookstore chain, Bookwell; and the department store chain will be called Gregory's.

These five organizations received intensive scrutiny. Interviews were

3

conducted with 62 of their members; a questionnaire survey was distributed to all 50 librarians; analyses were carried out on the titles the production and outlet organizations released during approximately the same period. These activities revealed that the different client relationships within the mass market and library market segments of children's book publishing have brought about deeply rooted, systemic consequences that cause markedly different book production and distribution policies in each segment, resulting in very different spectra of choice. Moreover, despite important differences between the segments, the same client relationship dynamics could be seen to operate in both areas. Consequently, generalizations about the influence of client relationships upon the production of mass media content could be formulated, generalizations that can be tested in further research. In order to best understand those findings and generalizations, the particulars of theory and method behind the research must first be reviewed.

THE CONCEPTUAL BACKGROUND

The consequences of different patron/producer interactions for the production of content directed towards the same purported general audience within the same mass media complex have never been investigated. It has been found, however, that factors other than the ultimate audience are often most immediately important to those people within the mass media production organizations responsible for the selection of content, even though audience images may occasionally play a significant background role.[3] In actuality, organizational goals and requirements, colleague and coworker rapport and pressures, the need to routinize tasks, and technological and logistical constraints become more salient than the interests of the audience.

While such findings are quite important for the light they can shed upon some of the determinants of content, their frames of analysis are not designed to focus upon the influences that shape these organizational constraints. Essentially, they ignore the fact that mass media production organizations fundamentally operate in an environment consisting of many other organizations. Beyond the study of an individual job within a mass media production organization, such as a publishing firm, and the relationships among several positions to the process of content selection, is the larger question of the influences that have shaped the organization's structure and decision making process. To understand how organizations are structured and how they carry out their activities, their relationships with the environment must be studied, a task few researchers have attempted. Studies that have scrutinized extraorganizational influences upon

4

mass media production organizations to some degree tend to lack a theoretical focus that will suggest the possibility of generalizing some of the findings to other mass media complexes.[4] Allied to this failing has been a failure to conduct, insofar as possible, comparative analyses of mass media complexes with the objective of determining how different characteristics within otherwise similar complexes influence the production of content, its distribution, and the final spectrum of choice presented to consumers.

Conceptual frameworks for such comparative analyses are not totally lacking. Developers of these frameworks seek to systematically attack several fundamental and surprisingly stubborn questions regarding the social context of symbol production, such as: Who produces society's shared messages? What biases of selection make the messages that are produced and distributed through an industry different from those that are not? What political and economic factors influence the content of cultural products and the audiences to which they are directed? Hirsch, for example, urges that an "industry system" perspective be used to "trace the flow of new products and ideas as they are filtered at each level of [mass media] organization."[5] Gerbner, in reviewing "institutional pressures on mass communicators," focuses attention on the continual interactions between a constellation of influential groups that participate in the production and distribution of content. Gerbner's use of the term "client relationship" to describe the most influential of these interactions has, as previously mentioned, been adopted for this investigation.[6]

Client relationships can be said to vary in their degree of patron influence. A major client relationship within a mass media complex refers to an interaction between a producer and its most important group of patron organizations. Because of the importance of such patrons to the producer's solvency, one might suspect that major client relationships would have substantial influence upon the structure and decision making process of the production organization. If this were valid, it would follow that two different client relationships would influence the production of different varieties of mass media content—even if the purported audience were the same in both cases.

THE CHILDREN'S BOOK COMPLEX

The general book complex that produces and distributes children's literature in America provides a suitable area in which to explore this hypothesis because, unlike most media complexes, it contains two distinct segments with separate, generally nonoverlapping client relationships, and the same purported audience. As noted earlier, the library market segment contains publishers who sell the overwhelming majority of their books to school and public (in other words, nonschool) libraries. In contrast, the mass market segment contains publishers who market their books overwhelmingly to a large variety of nonlibrary outlets—particularly discount, department, and book stores. The library market distribution outlets generally contain publicly sponsored selectors—librarians—who purchase the books, both fiction and nonfiction, from which the audience may ultimately choose. In the mass market segment this function is performed by privately sponsored agents—buyers—from such outlets as department, discount, and book stores, as well as from outlet servicers such as jobbers and wholesalers. It should be emphasized that mass market distribution outlets stock relatively few library market books and libraries stock relatively few mass market materials. This separation obtains at the publishing level as well: mass market publishers are rarely also library market publishers and vice versa.

Another important characteristic of the children's book complex should be recalled at this point: the patrons of the publishing firms in each segment are also the ultimate distributors of their books to the readers. In essence, then, an examination of the client relationships within the mass market and library market areas of the children's book industry would be an examination of the influences upon the selection of mass media material at two levels—that of the producer and that of the distribution outlet.[7]

Statistical Information

Investigation of current literature on children's books reveals little concern with the organizational questions raised in the previous section. In fact, no sources attempt to even delineate the children's book complex in terms of the books produced and distributed; that is, no study can be found that tries to break down the relative sales of, the number of books produced for, and the number of books distributed in the library market, the mass market, the home book club, and the school book club markets that make up the complex. The available statistics must be culled from what little research there is on the general market for books, and these figures are invariably selective or estimated, since some publishers refuse to divulge their sales figures.

Table 1 presents data compiled for the Association of American Publishers (AAP) that estimate book publishing industry sales by AAP survey categories. The figures found under "juvenile" do not include either home or school book club sales; almost no public information is available with regard to those two segments. The juvenile statistics in table 1 thus refer

TABLE 1

Estimated Trade Book Publishing Industry Sales
by AAP Survey Categories (Millions of Dollars)

	1973	1974	1975	1976	1976 Percent Change From '75	1976 Percent Change From '71
TRADE (TOTAL)	460.1	522.7	549.2	573.3	4.4	35.6
Adult Hardbound	264.8	308.2	313.4	331.0	5.6	36.8
Adult Paperbound	86.7	97.3	111.2	117.8	5.9	69.3
Juvenile Hardbound	98.8	103.1	109.6	109.1	—.5	.2
Juvenile Paperbound*	9.8	14.1	15.0	17.4	16.0	690.9

*These figures probably do not include paperbacks in "mass market" (small) format. The AAP categories do not provide information on sales in that area.

Source: *Publishers Weekly,* August 22, 1977, p. 38.

to the library and mass markets. Unfortunately, however, the 109.1 million dollars worth of juvenile book sales that is reported for 1976 does not include the sales of an extremely important mass market juvenile book producer, Western Publishing, which is not a member of the AAP. Moreover, the nature of the survey report is such that an AAP member might have reported its adult but not its juvenile sales. Because of the fiercely competitive nature of the juvenile mass market, such a failure to report is a distinct possibility. Indeed, the sales manager of an important mass market firm speculated to this writer that his company did not report its juvenile sales to AAP. It must thus be concluded that table 1 seriously underestimates total juvenile sales.

The AAP statistics do not allow for a clear differentiation between the library and mass market segments; nor does any other study follow juvenile books from publishers to outlets in an attempt to accurately note the size of each segment and the degree to which they are distinct. A conception of the magnitude of sales to school and public libraries can, however, be found in a study of the library market commissioned by *Publishers Weekly.*[8] This study, the latest to be conducted, estimates that during the 1974–75 school year, school libraries bought 46.2 million dollars worth of juvenile books and public libraries bought 32.9 million dollars worth. These figures cannot be strictly compared to the AAP total estimate of 117.8 million presented earlier because of the somewhat different time frames used; the difference of 38.7 million dollars can only, in any event, be taken as a rough estimate of book sales to classrooms combined with some of the sales to the mass market.

Unfortunately, no report of the number of children's books printed in the mid-1970s could be found. It is known that approximately 3,000 new children's book titles were published in America during each year and that 85 percent of these were destined for school and public libraries.[9] The general number of children's books that have been circulating through American school and public libraries in recent years is not available. This figure would be most appropriately compared to the number of units sold in the mass market to gauge the relative number of children who are being reached in both segments. The most recent statistic of this sort, compiled in 1962, shows that the total number of juvenile books circulated during that year through public libraries serving over 35,000 people (there were 860 such libraries) was 215,594,239.[10] Although this figure and others previously presented do not really contribute specifications regarding the size and reach of the mass market segments in the mid-1970s, they do give a general idea of the magnitude of both those areas.

Writing and Research

Statistical information on the children's book complex is, obviously, lacking. Literature on the operation of publishing firms in the complex, though available, is not very extensive and does not speak to the concerns of the present study. One text devoted entirely to the children's book field, Jean Colby's *Writing, Illustrating, and Editing Children's Books* is, despite its age, a handy introduction to the routines of the trade. However, Colby is almost exclusively interested in library market books, and the influence of client relationships even in this segment is not one of her concerns.

Of the general guides to book publishing, only the anthologies by Grannis and Kujoth deal with juvenile publishing in any detail.[11] In the former book, an especially interesting article by Karl presents an overview of the basic activities involved in producing and marketing children's books and devotes several paragraphs to the differences between mass market and library market juveniles, noting that quick sales and high-powered merchandising by subject and publisher names are the hallmarks and fortes of the mass market.[12] Lanes, in a wide-ranging, generally literary analysis of children's literature, also distinguishes between the two markets; she praises the library market products as creative and condemns mass market output as hackneyed and nonliterary.[13]

The amount of sociological research conducted on the publishing industry in general has also been quite small, although there is a growing recognition of the importance of this area as a field of study. In the September, 1975, issue of *The Annals,* devoted entirely to book publishing (mostly of the academic and scholarly sort), Lewis Coser commented that "curiously enough, no major sociological study of the modern publishing industry is available."[14] One of the few published pieces of research about the children's book industry does, however, touch upon the importance of the client relationships for the library market. William Jenkins, in a 1964 survey of children's book editors, found that the editors, when asked to rank "the factors affecting publishers' decisions to publish a given children's title," tended to place "librarians' requests or comments" and "teachers requests or comments" first and second, while "market analyses of children's reading habits," "patterns in adult reading habits," "trends in other mass media," and "publishing trends in other countries" were ranked sixth through last, respectively.[15] Unfortunately, no published updating or extension of this study could be found.

No research at all could be found regarding mass market outlets for children's books; the greatest amount of writing about the children's book complex undoubtedly concerns the selection of particular books for public and school libraries. Magazines such as *School Library Journal, The Horn Book, Publishers Weekly,* and others evaluate many new titles for juveniles in every issue, primarily as an aid to librarians in choosing books for their shelves. *Virginia Kirkus Reviews, Booklist,* and *Bulletin of the Center for Children's Books* are major reviewing operations aimed at critiquing an enormous number of children's books for the benefit of subscribing librarians. The *New York Times Book Review,* with a more general audience, publishes weekly reviews of a few juvenile titles. Most of the reviews in these media are short statements about the quality of a given book and its appropriateness for children at certain age or grade levels. Lengthier pieces of reflective literary criticism are rarer but can be found in such journals as *The Horn Book, Bookbird, Phaedrus, Language Arts,* and *College English* and in the works of such critics as John Rowe Townsend.[16] Articles on book selection regularly appear in the trade press and in productions of more radical voices such as the *Carnegie Quarterly, Interracial Books for Children Bulletin, Feminists on Children's Media,* and *Women on Words and Images.* Some of the trade articles have been collected in anthologies.[17]

Most of those who write on children's books would probably agree with the concern which Weitzman and her colleagues evidenced regarding this mass medium:

Through books, children learn about the world outside of their immediate environment; they learn what other boys and girls do, say, and feel; they learn about what is right and wrong; and they learn what is expected of their age. In addition, books provide children with role models—images of what they can and should be.[18]

General guidelines for the selection of children's books that reflect this concern can be found in introductory texts on library work with children[19] and in works on the world of children's literature.[20] When discussing selection, these books basically articulate a view of children and childhood and then provide generalizations about the types of books that should be chosen for different ages so that, in the words of one writer, they "will find in the library sources for everlasting growth, wonder, and delight."[21]

Most studies of library selection are surveys directed toward the question of library censorship, a sanction that is only one facet of the overall organizational selection process.[22] Moreover, of the seven studies mentioned above, only Marjorie Fiske's research was conducted through interviews; the rest used questionnaires and concentrated on quantifiable conclusions about opinions of large librarian populations rather than on the particular pressures that influence them. Fiske's sixteen-year-old study contains many important and interesting insights into the pressures on librarians. However, it suffers somewhat from the fact that the interviews were conducted with head librarians and school principals only, rather than the rank and file who select books for the branches, as well as from her failure to confront squarely the meaning of censorship. In addition, Fiske mentions children's books only incidentally.

RESEARCH AND METHODOLOGY

Because the aim of this investigation was to compare the consequences of different client relationships on the selection of content at production and distribution outlet levels of the library and mass markets, a case study approach that allowed for in-depth organizational analysis was used. Production and distribution outlet organizations from the library market and mass market were studied. The goal was to chart the influences upon the selectors of content within each organization and, extensionally, to gauge the impact of client relationships on various aspects of book selection at both the production and distribution levels.

Both publishing firms studied are large corporations with children's book divisions known to have strong sales and good reputations in their chosen primary marketplaces. R&A Publishing orients its children's books toward

10

the library market, while Global Publishing directs its children's books primarily toward the mass market. Strictly speaking, these large firms cannot be considered typical of the companies in their segments. The 48 library market publishers who are members of the Children's Book Council range in size from operations with a single editor and a few assistants to firms with several editors, editorial assistants, and publicity personnel. In the mass market arena, large companies do predominate; of the 6 firms oriented to book and department stores, 4 are publishing giants. The decision to study large firms that are important in their segments was made for two reasons. First, it was thought that such firms might have particularly influential interactions with their outlets that might be important to observe. Second, and more important, it was felt that scrutiny of a large publisher in the library market was necessary to make reasonable comparisons with the mass market segment, where the most prominent publishers are giants.

Public libraries that provide service to children also vary in size, as do commercial outlets selling children's books. Libraries range from one-room setups, in which the same librarian chooses and shelves all the books for children, to hierarchically structured organizations that employ numerous librarians and service millions of children. Commercial outlets range in type from large supermarkets to small bookshops. As in the case of the publishers, it is impossible to find outlet organizations that are typical of outlets in the mass market and library market segments. Consequently— and consistently—the decision was to choose outlets in terms of influence. The library that was studied—Metrosystem—is located in an eastern American city and ranks as one of the top 10 public systems in the country in terms of circulation, expense, and staff size.[23] In the commercial sphere, both a bookstore chain and a department store chain were chosen for examination because of an initial feeling that bookstores might have very different requirements and selection guidelines than any other kinds of mass market outlets. Like the other organizations, the two chains are extremely prominent in their areas of operation. The bookstore chain— Bookwell—operates many stores throughout the country, including 4 in the area studied, and the department store—Gregory's—is a nationally known regional chain with 11 branches in the area studied. The library system, the bookstore chain, and the department store chain were all chosen from the same city so that the consequences of the different client relationships for distribution of a sizable number of juvenile books within the same area could be examined. It is also important to point out that while these cases cannot be termed typical, supplementary interviews carried out with individuals throughout the children's book complex have shown that there are enough structural and procedural similarities common to the members

11

of each segment to allow an inference that the relations among organizations as described in this book hold true for the entire children's book complex.

The focus of a large part of the research was on those positions in each organization that have responsibility for determining the books to be accepted. People in such positions can be designated as production or outlet selectors, depending on whether they belong to production or outlet organizations. The number of relevant selectors in the publishing firms of both segments and in the mass market distribution outlet organizations was small enough so that an attempt could be made to interview all of them. However, the large number of branch librarians (45) necessitated the distribution of questionnaires to them after 15 (and 4 library coordinators) were interviewed. The Appendix goes into some detail about the specifics of interviewing and of the questionnaire survey.

In order to obtain a broader understanding of the environment in which the chosen firms are operating, one which helps shape their operation, this comparative case study was supplemented by interviews with key figures from throughout both segments of the complex and by a historical analysis of the origin of the client relationships. Although this book cannot possibly deal at length with the history of the children's book industry, it can provide a short overview of the profound influence the emerging client relationships had on the development of the entire children's book complex and, by extension, on the organizations chosen for this investigation.

PREVIEW

The parts and chapters that follow will delve into the particulars of this study and explore its findings. Part 1 will deal with the consequences of the major client relationship in the library market segment. The preface outlines the historical origins of the relationship; chapter 2 examines the publishing organization; and chapter 3 discusses the distribution outlet. The preface for part 2 and two chapters will do the same for the mass market segment and will compare the findings with those in the library market. A concluding chapter will summarize and explain major findings, comment on their ramifications, and suggest directions for further investigation.

Part 1

The Library Market

Chapter 1: A Historical Preface

A comprehensive chronicle of the children's book industry in America has yet to be written. However, historical surveys are adequate for tracing, at least in bold outline, the origin of the major client relationship that exists between libraries and large groups of publishing firms with regard to juvenile books. The development of this relationship can be seen as a culmination of the public library movement for children in the late nineteenth and early twentieth centuries.

Isolated examples of public libraries for American youth existed as early as 1803, when Caleb Bingham, a bookseller, donated a library to his town of Salisbury, Connecticut, for use by children ages 9 to 16.[1] The need for public library service to children was not generally recognized during the first three quarters of the nineteenth century, however, even though the adult public library movement was making impressive progress. As late as 1890, the great majority of public libraries barred everyone below the ages of 12 or 14; some even posted notices reading "no dogs or children admitted."[2] During this period of neglect, the agency that reached more children than any other was the Sunday school, which provided books considered suitable for children to read. From the beginning of the nineteenth century, such once-a-week schools circulated material on a reward system; pupils who had shown good behavior or attendance received tickets to borrow books that were to be returned the following week. The first Sunday schools demanded tracts of a highly religious, moral character for their libraries, and general book publishers did not seem interested in supplying books of this nature. Consequently, the American Sunday School Union, an umbrella organization, undertook the publication of what came to be known as the "Sunday school book" of the nineteenth century—"a type of book filled with evangelical zeal and sentimentality."[3] Different denominational publishing firms also contributed to the output. In 1831 the American Sunday School Union could boast of 300 volumes for every Sunday school in the United States.[4]

The character of the Sunday school book collections changed as the years passed, with the general tenor becoming somewhat more secular.[5] By 1870 the union no longer existed, and Sunday school librarians were turning to the open market to purchase their books. This development—and the juvenile literacy that the public and Sunday school movements had spawned—precipitated a flood of quarto children's picture books such that, in 1889, one bookmaker complained that the quartos were being manufactured at so small a margin of profit that it scarcely paid to promote them. He stated that they were meant only for the cheapest market, the drygoods counter, where they were selling for anywhere from 25 to 60 cents, scarcely ever going as high as a dollar. The competition in bookstores and other outlets was so savage that the larger houses, forced into the field, were barely holding their ground.[6]

Sunday school librarians, usually with no training in book selection, were not judged competent to select wisely from among the materials available. Harriet Long notes that "a few of the religious denominations sought to remedy the situation by issuing approved buying lists, but Sunday School librarians, even so, were easy prey. Some of them, indeed, would simply send an order for so many dollars worth of books to some leading publisher, leaving the selection to his judgment or interest. Book collections were also often augmented by gifts when families weeded out their home libraries."[7]

PUBLIC LIBRARY SERVICE FOR CHILDREN

At the same time that the Sunday school libraries were experiencing selection problems and the publishing community was in turmoil over the number and prices of juvenile books, a movement to establish children's rooms in public libraries, with supervision and book selection to be carried out by professionals, was gaining momentum. This movement eventually caused the gradual disappearance of the Sunday school library and created a relatively stable, predictable market for materials, allowing some publishers to escape the savage competition brought by the recent inundation of juvenile titles.

In 1894 Lutie Stearns of the Milwaukee Public Library presented a report at the American Library Association conference that detailed the paucity of adequate library service for children. She is credited with creating a clear conviction among the librarians present that age limitation should be abolished in the public library, and that special rooms for children, with special attendants designated to serve children, should be provided.[8] In 1896 Anne Carroll Moore introduced lectures (and, later, a course) on library work with children at Brooklyn's Pratt Institute, an activity emulated in other library schools. In 1898 Francis Jenkins Olcott organized the first children's coordinating department in a public library—the Carnegie Library of Pittsburgh—and developed a pattern for reaching children through the children's rooms of branch libraries, schools, and through the homes. Other such departments followed; with their creation came the establishment of policies and objectives, the determination of criteria for book selection, and the development of work methods. In the words of Elizabeth Nesbitt, "as the twentieth century approached the end of its second decade, library work with children had become an important and established phase of public library work."[9]

THE QUIET REVOLUTION

Thus, by the end of the 1920s, the stage was set for what John Tebbel has called "the quiet revolution in children's book publishing."[10] Until that time, publishing firms had been handling children's books as part of their adult trade activity; no special effort had been made to create a juvenile department with a separate identity and line. The increasing number of juvenile libraries requiring an increasing number of books that would meet their selection objectives and guidelines encouraged such a development, however. In 1918 the Macmillan Company pioneered in creating a Children's Book Department with Louise Seaman, a former schoolteacher and an employee of the firm, as its head. In 1922 May Massee, a librarian and editor of *The Booklist* (published by the American Library Association), became the first children's book editor at Doubleday, Page, and Company; Marion Fiery, from Anne Carroll Moore's department at the New York Public Library, was appointed to that position at E. P. Dutton three years later. Other companies followed, and by 1928, a decade after the Seaman appointment, eight publishing houses had juvenile divisions.[11] Ensuing years brought many more.

The flavor of the client relationship that developed between publishing houses with juvenile divisions and public libraries is reflected in the reminiscences of the distinguished children's book editor, Margaret K. McElderry:

> Before entering the publishing profession, I had been a fascinated observer of children's books from a rather special vantage point. A beginning children's librarian just when the country was starting to pull out of the Depression, I first worked in the office of Anne Carroll Moore, who had been, since the inception of the position in 1906, Director of Work With Children in The New York Public Library. As junior assistant, I reported ten minutes before opening time each day to dust, sharpen pencils, and

17

straighten—but never to rearrange—the great piles of papers and books on Miss Moore's desk. Into Room 105, as the office was known, came almost everyone interested in or connected with children's books—editors, authors, illustrators, reviewers, educators, and librarians—seeking advice or imparting information. Since Miss Moore's desk was separated from the rest of the office only by a leather screen, it was impossible not to hear nearly everything that went on—though one would sometimes have preferred not to.

The children's book editors who came were, with a few exceptions, those who had first established children's book departments. . . .

In retrospect, it is clear that one of the great strengths of children's book publishing has been the stability and continuity of its leadership. Strong-minded, dedicated women they were, all of them. (Until 1935, when Vernon Ives and Holiday House arrived on the scene, there were no male editors of books for children.) . . . The precepts and principles they established—and, in most cases, continued to practice for years to come— provided the strong foundation on which children's book publishing still stands.

. . . These editors and librarians naturally formed strong friendships of great mutual benefit. Such a relationship has never existed to any degree between adult editors and librarians. It continues to be a particular strength of the children's publishing and library world.[12]

THE RELATIONSHIP TODAY

The children's publishing and library world has changed considerably since the early 1930s. In 1977 the Children's Book Council, an organization of publishers that sell primarily to libraries, had 52 members. Moreover, the types of libraries important to the publishers had broadened. In the days of the first juvenile divisions, the principal patrons within the children's library market were the public libraries. School libraries were too few and too weak to have much influence. By the late 1960s, however, school libraries had become powerful elements in the client relationship, a development precipitated largely as a result of the 1965 federal Elementary and Secondary Education Act, which made available one billion dollars for school library materials, textbooks, and other instructional materials.[13] Although this funding was cut drastically during the early 1970s, the broadened client base remained. By 1977 the number of school and public libraries in the United States had reached 83,953.[14] Margaret McElderry's remarks indicate that although the library market segment of children's book publishing has changed since the days of the quiet revolution, the major client relationship has been institutionalized

18

and its surface manifestations—the interactions between editors and librarians—are generally recognized as an integral part of the juvenile library market. Even the large scale introduction of paperback reprints of popular juvenile library titles into classrooms, book fairs, some bookstores, and some department stores (as well as into libraries)—an activity initiated by nonjuvenile publisher Dell in the late 1960s—has done little to change the essential focuses of the library market client relationship, though it has broadened the availability of that relationship's product.

The following two chapters will explore the consequences of the library market client relationship for one publishing firm and one public library system within the library market segment, showing that the impact of the major client relationship reaches to the core of the publishing operation by structuring—and thus delimiting—the range of necessary and desired activities for a publishing firm when it chooses, produces, promotes, and markets books for the library market. Similarly, though perhaps more subtly, the relationship will be shown as having strong and important influences upon the public library system, both in terms of reinforcing certain library market prespectives towards children's books championed by the dominant publishers, and in terms of perpetuating the power of those firms to set new trends and define important issues for the system's librarians.

Chapter 2:   The Library Market
Publisher

R&A Publishing, the library market firm used in this study, is a very large company operating under a "federal system" of publishing, wherein different divisions—adult, trade, juvenile, college, medical, adult paperback, and international—are held responsible for the discovery, production, and marketing of their own books. Under such an arrangement, the firm's top management oversees the financial condition of each division, apportions the yearly budgets, and initiates or oversees major policy or price changes. Day to day operations and decisions, however, are carried out by the divisional publisher and staff.

R&A began publishing children's books over a century ago as part of its regular trade book activity, and its specialized Children's Book Division was founded relatively early in the quiet revolution. That division is recognized today as one of the sales leaders within the juvenile book industry and is widely respected throughout the library market for its output.

Like all library market firms, the overwhelming percentage of R&A's children's book sales is to school and public libraries. According to the company's marketing director, 85 percent of R&A's hardbound books for children end up in the institutional arena. However, the division is unusual in that a fair number of its hardbound titles, mostly those which have already gained popularity in the library, can be found in bookstores. Also, a significant minority of its juvenile paperbacks (reprints of some R&A hardbacks) have been getting into both book and department stores.

The Children's Book Division is treated as a separate entity on R&A's organizational chart. The division has its own publisher, production manager, assistant production manager, and production staff. The division also has its own sales manager, but shares a marketing department, consisting of promotion, sales, and publicity sections, with the adult trade book division. R&A's marketing director explained that this arrangement is most efficient, since the divisions share essentially the same marketplace— libraries and bookstores. The juvenile paperbacks are represented by sales-

20

people from the adult paperback division as well as by the trade marketing force.

Among the direct selectors of children's books are four different positions: the publisher, who oversees the division; four senior editors, who choose manuscripts and guide them to completion; four associate editors who, less experienced than the senior editors, perform the same tasks, but with more oversight from the publisher and senior editors; and three readers, who read and critique all manuscripts arriving at the division before they are sent for further consideration to the editors or associate editors. It should be stressed that the R&A children's publisher is also an editor. While this situation seems to hold true in federally organized publishing firms throughout the library market, such is not the case in the mass market, as will be seen. The significance of this and other structural variances will have to await a direct comparison of the library market and mass market firms. Here will only be noted the fact that the differences to be found are intimately related to—and reflective of—the different activities shaped by the client relationship in each segment.

The more immediate task is to explore the consequences of the selectors' continual interaction with librarians for the process and product of children's book publishing. This task must logically begin with an examination of the manner in which R&A selectors conceptualize the signal requirements and opportunities of their major client relationship.

THE CLIENT RELATIONSHIP

The significance of libraries and librarians to the continued economic well-being of R&A was well understood by everyone interviewed. "Librarians are extremely important to us because libraries of all kinds constitute the major markets for our books," noted one editor, when asked about her contacts with representatives of their distribution outlets. The publisher, essentially saying the same thing, phrased it in terms of the ultimate spectrum of choice presented to the readers: "Librarians are very important to us because they are the ones who bring books to children."

This realization of the bottom-line importance of libraries and librarians has naturally led selectors to attempt to understand their major market and its operations with respect to R&A. Remarks made by subjects interviewed about the factors influencing their activities revealed an underlying conception of crucial requirements and opportunities that are mandated by the division's dealings with clients. Further analysis shows that this conception has itself been shaped by three major considerations: (1) The tradition of the publishing house and the proclivities of the division's direct selectors; (2) the environment of selection in, and economic nature of, the marketplace; and (3) the environment for response and promotion. The following sections will outline these considerations and show how they interrelate and merge to form a conception of the major requirements and opportunities posed by the library market client relationship.

The Tradition of the House

A strong pride in R&A's tradition regarding children's books seemed to mesh well with the proclivities of the editors within the organization. Both an editor and a salesperson referred to the presence of several R&A books on a list of the best children's books of all time; a reader spoke reverentially of a selection policy that had been set by an early R&A children's publisher. The editors and reader could also be seen to pride themselves on the editorial control exercised by their division. Interviewed subjects from throughout the firm agreed that the Children's Book Division is freer from the interference of R&A marketing and sales personnel than any other division within the company. A related thread running through the comments of all the direct selectors was the desire to publish books that are departures from the ordinary. An editor summed up these feelings well:

> We love to do something fresh. We don't do it just for novelty's sake. We do it because we like it. If somebody comes up with a fresh idea, it's wonderful. We would like to consider ourselves doing innovative books. They're the most fun to do. But we do a mix. We do all kinds of books.

A specific heritage from the past was tied to activities of the present by an associate editor, who explained that the division tends to publish mostly fiction partly because it has a tradition of strength in that area, and partly because most of the current editors are partial to fiction. This preference was admitted by all the interviewed editors, though the publisher followed the admission with the statement that the division's commitment was actually, and of greater importance, to what she and the other selectors consistently characterized as "good books." (The guidelines by which the R&A personnel define good books and quality will be discussed later.)

The Marketplace

The R&A selectors presented a view of their marketplace that emphasized the prudence of their book publishing perspective from the standpoint of sales. The editors, reader, and marketing director were quick to indicate that the librarians, who must pass their books, are professionals who want to introduce high quality titles to children and to create a library environment favorable to the selection of good books. "It's my impression they'd like good books, you know, and the more good books the better," R&A's promotion director remarked when asked about the types of books desired by outlets that are not being published.

The R&A selectors also responded to economic considerations with their clients in mind. The general consensus among the selectors regarding book prices was that increases in costs of supplies and manufacturing have made higher prices inevitable but that, in the words of an associate editor, "right now there isn't much price resistance on the part of librarians." The promotion director, agreeing, contended that in times of budgetary crises and limited book-buying funds, a library's first priority is for "what they think is very good," not for what is inexpensive. When asked if he thought librarians' need for good books ever conflicted with a need for popular books, the director responded in the following manner: "Well, Dr. Seuss has never been terribly popular with librarians even though he's popular otherwise. See, since at least 80 percent of our business is to the institutional market we've always tried to combine popularity with quality."

The need to produce books that are popular with librarian-buyers is a requirement that echoed through the remarks of all the interviewed personnel. A few of the editors also pointed out that they are concerned about the circulation of their books among children once they get onto the shelf, since librarians continually rebuy titles as books become worn, are stolen, or lost. In fact, they said, the general library policy of replacing worn books that are considered worthwhile has made a company's backlist of titles very important in juvenile book publishing. Personnel from throughout the library market were in agreement that the backlist tends to be the steadiest and most lucrative source of a juvenile division's income. The R&A editors were quick to point out, however, that simply imitating past successes is a sure way to failure, since librarians shun formulaic material, even if the original was considered a good book. Thus, the R&A selectors implied, the client relationship encourages a predilection for fresh ideas.

The Environment for Response and Promotion

The R&A selectors' understanding of the environment in which they receive responses about old books and promote new ones made them more secure in their ability to successfully publish fresh, innovative literature. That environment encompasses both direct and indirect avenues of contact with the library world. Indirect avenues include review media and journals, which provide information about trends, grants, and activities, as well as book critiques and advertisements. Direct avenues include the interactions of the division's publicity director, promotion director, and seven-person promotion staff with librarians and library school teachers (who form the opinions of incipient librarians), both where they work and at conferences. The directors write periodic reports of their impressions and attend the division's weekly editorial meetings, in which new editorial and promotional ideas are often discussed. The editors themselves sometimes attend library conferences, often to appear on discussion panels or give addresses.

Note that the thrust of the promotional and feedback activities are aimed at the librarians, not at the purported ultimate audience. R&A's marketing director stated that the division simply does not have the money to advertise or promote its books heavily through the general mass media to parents or children. Since librarians are by far the major purchasers, they are the major targets to be reached with any available funds. And, indeed, the avenues of contact with the library world serve a dual purpose for R&A. From the standpoint of feedback, they allow the editors and promotion people to keep in touch with trends in circulation, librarian interest, and librarian perception of children's abilities—and to use that knowledge when selecting manuscripts. The promotion director was emphatic in underscoring that his input into the editorial process is strictly informational. When asked about his influence regarding the selection of particular content characteristics listed on the interview schedule, the director consistently answered "not influential" and, when asked about the subject of the book, stated:

> I really don't have any say. I think that one reason that [R&A] has such a good reputation is that they [i.e., the editors] take the books which they feel are the best. And nothing is to order here. I would no more presume going up and saying "We've gotta have some books on such and such a subject"—and they'd tell me to go to Hell!

The tenor of all the R&A interviews tended to support the promotion director's remarks. In fact, that director and an editor specifically pointed out that acquaintance with librarians and knowledge about their needs are often more forcefully and specifically used by the division to promote books, rather than to select them. Through the distribution of catalogs, R&A subject booklists, trade ads; through selective circulation of complimentary copies of new books to influential librarians and library systems; through the frequent promulgation to conference audiences by R&A editors (and editors from similarly inclined publishing firms) of their perspectives on books and book publishing; through the visiting of library systems by R&A authors and illustrators; and through the friendly and close relationships between publishing people on the one hand and leading librarians and library school teachers on the other, a favorable environment for the reception of the division's books is created.

24

Routine promotion sometimes gives way to more intense promotion of particular titles agreed upon by promotion and editorial people, as in the case of the prestigious and monetarily significant Caldecott and Newbery awards. One editor pointed out that acquaintances with important librarians can also be efficacious in facilitating the acceptance of a particularly novel or avant garde R&A title, or in getting libraries to publicize among children an important project connected to R&A, such as a film version of a division book. The mentioning of such capabilities, also done by another editor and the promotion director, signifies the belief that the publishing community (and even an individual, prestigious house such as R&A) can initiate new trends and, within limits, shape the view of the library community as to what constitutes a good book.

Note that the cultivation by R&A of a reputation for producing good books and always searching for fresh ideas might also help the firm's titles that are designed to capitalize on trends not considered particularly imaginative or innovative. Most of the subjects preferred to dwell on the most creative aspect of their work, indicating their predilection for this area— and, perhaps, the influence of the promotional stance upon their responses.

SELECTING AND PRODUCING BOOKS
FOR THE LIBRARY MARKET

The previous discussion shows that the R&A selectors understand that the demands and opportunities of their client relationship encourages a particular approach towards their selection and publication of books. In the following sections, the selectors' understanding of the client relationship will be shown to have consequences for the firm's actual publishing process as well—from the responsibilities and activities of the principals involved to their guidelines regarding the formulation of seasonal lists and the choosing of titles.

Influences on the Selectors

Several subtle influences made by the client relationship upon the responsibilities and activities of the editors and reader are effectively highlighted through a comparison of the mass market and library market publishing firms, a task carried out in part 2. One responsibility of the principals involved in the selection of titles for R&A that can be immediately connected to the client relationship, however, is the editorial autonomy of the children's division from the firm's trade marketing and sales departments. In view of the close connections between the editors, their small promotion staff, and the library market, as well as the absence of any substantial role of the firm's trade sales force (since the librarians order the books themselves directly from institutional jobbers), it is easy to understand why the Children's Book Division is allowed to be so independent.

Another broad responsibility on the part of the R&A selectors that stems from their perceptions of demands and opportunities in the client relationship is their commitment to read every manuscript and examine every illustration offered to the house for publication. This commitment, with broad implications for the book selection process, was described as a logical extension of the selectors' commitment and requirement to uncover untapped writing and illustrating talent.

A chief mechanism for uncovering new soures of good books is the group of three readers, who read all of the approximately 6,000 manuscripts received yearly, including those by previously published authors, and refer them to an editor with critiques and recommendations for acceptance or rejection. The interviewed reader stressed the egalitarian image created by this policy, and the exciting serendipity it injects into the manuscript reviewing process:

> ... We try to give equal chance to everyone—housewives, husbands, whatever comes in. [A former publisher of the division] used to take great pride in this. In a way, it's more exciting to discover someone unknown. I shouldn't say discover. That's too pompous. But to discover something new! And, also, an astonishing number of young people—particularly artists—come in all the time. We used to have someone who interviewed artists—an editor who has a little more knowledge about that area would do that. But now artists just make appointments with various editors. And there's an incredible number of young people who are gifted. I mean, 18 year olds, 17 year olds. And they bring their portfolios and we keep them on hand, and if a book comes along that's right for them, we use them.

A major aim of such an all-inclusive review, one carried out in many library market firms, is undoubtedly promotional—to show librarians that the division is indeed actively searching for the best in children's literature wherever it can find it. However, one editor pointed to somewhat more concrete demands of the marketplace for going to such great lengths to review books: because the vogues of children's fiction in the library market are quite changeable, because the emphasis is on new directions as well as on replacing old books, an editor is expected to cultivate new writers and illustrators and, in the process, to help ensure that the division's overall backlist will continue to be filled with writers and illustrators whose books circulate in the libraries and who have a reputation for quality. It might be noted that the burden of discovering new faces falls particularly upon the newer, associate editors, who feel obliged to search for new names because, unlike some of the senior staff, they are not comfortably ensconced with still-popular old ones.

The Cultivation of Talent

As the preceding paragraph implies, the introduction of new writers and illustrators—and especially writer-illustrators of picture books—is usually a time-consuming process. Although subjects both in R&A and in other firms agreed that attention by review media and librarians to books by new talent makes it easier in the juvenile than in the adult trade book market to succeed with a critically lauded first work of fiction, none seemed willing to count on such quick success. One R&A editor stated that the division will rarely publish only one book by a new author, even if it loses money and doesn't draw acclaim; moreover, she said that the organization might even publish a mediocre first book if the editor and publisher feel the creator has potential. When they decide to launch a relationship with an unknown writer, she explained, they do so with an eye towards the future, towards helping that person develop his or her ʻalent and become an important figure in the library world.

The decision to use an unknown illustrator, though perhaps not involving such long-term commitment, does, however, involve risk. One particularly vexing problem with regard to novice illustrators is the question of whether they can satisfactorily perform the difficult technical and artistic tasks demanded of them, including hand-separation of colors with a 3-color picture book, in coordination with the publishing time schedule. Delays in this area can add substantially to a book's costs. An additional danger—the raiding of artists by competitors—was pointed out by an associate editor: "It's quite risky. We get ripped off a lot. We take the risk, and then other people use our artists."

While the amount of time and energy that the cultivation of new talent consumes does not encourage its frequency, the interviewed editors insisted they felt obliged to take chances on unknowns. One associate editor said that "every new list that we have seems to have a couple of new people, artists or authors." The most usual risk taken by R&A, however, is in the publishing of authors and illustrators who have published previously—either for other firms or for R&A. While illustrators tend not to be identified with particular houses and are pursued by editors who see their pictorial style and expertise as complementing a particular manuscript, writers and writer-illustrators generally stay with one publishing firm, usually because of the

27

relationship they have developed with an editor. In fact, often when an editor moves to another firm, he or she will take some "house authors" along.

The Cultivation of "Good Book" Ideas

The working relationship between an author and editor was seen by the direct selectors as an important contributor to new and successful works. No R&A editor admitted to conceptualizing a work of fiction and finding a house author to carry it out; such activity is not considered conducive to good books, although it is acceptable in nonfiction. However, two R&A editors did comment upon the importance of a continuing interaction between writers and their editors. Such closeness, one commented, "breeds new ideas." The editor, after receiving feedback about the types of subjects becoming popular among librarians, might guide an author in certain directions, encourage certain fresh ideas and discourage others. What makes this activity fruitfully interactive from the standpoint of the editors is that most experienced juvenile book writers have quite a facility for keeping up with the trends. One R&A editor recounted how she told an author that more books are needed on the Holocaust; the writer replied that he had, by chance, been intermittently working on a manuscript dealing with the subject. From that conversation came a completed book.

One general impression gained from interviews, conversations, and observations throughout the focal library market firm is that the more immersed an individual is in the environment of the library market segment and its literature, the more likely the person will be to get a book published. This need to understand the type of work desired for publication as a library market children's book, and the need to be in touch with the segment's ongoing literary tradition, is perhaps best expressed in the following comment by an R&A editor: "If I were giving advice, as I frequently do, to beginning authors, I would advise them to familiarize themselves with what is available in the library and what seems to have the most movement." Such an approach, particularly when combined with a close relationship with an editor, would seem to greatly increase the chance of producing a good manuscript that will be accepted for publication.

The Editorial Procedure

The R&A selectors' conviction that their marketplace demands titles with a fresh, nonformulaic stamp has been translated into their division's commitment to weigh all incoming manuscripts and illustrations for publication. Actually, the concrete consequences of this conviction extend beyond the initial screening of works. Consistently underlying the remarks of all R&A

editors was the notion that their primary focus is upon producing an "artistic creation," as one editor phrased it, a book in which all the elements make aesthetic as well as economic sense. The editors preferred to see themselves as working with individual titles or individual authors, rather than with certain book categories. Although every editor admitted to certain likes and dislikes with regard to developing manuscripts, all stressed a preference for working on different kinds of books to vary their routines and expand their creativity. Moreover, all agreed that the division's book selection procedure allows this freedom.

The R&A editorial book selection procedure takes place throughout the year. After their initial examination by a reader, all manuscripts, whether recommended for acceptance or not, are distributed by the manuscript supervisor to an editor or associate editor. If the editor decides to produce a book from the manuscript, he or she presents a case to the publisher, including a preliminary manufacturing estimate, which is a general evaluation of the cost of the book against its potential sales. When dealing with an unpublished author, potential sales might be gauged by examining sales of recent books on similar subjects by first-time authors. With an author whose work has been published previously by the house, the projection is considered to be more accurate. In either case, the sales manager and production director might be asked to lend their expertise to the estimate.

If the publisher's approval to sign the contract is forthcoming, the book is tentatively given a publication date (the year and season—spring or fall—that the title will be released) and the editor and author begin the intricacies and overlapping activities of the preproduction process. How long this process will take depends on the type of book under consideration and the stage it is at when the contract is signed. If the manuscript consists of only a few sample chapters or an outline, the writer, who may have received an advance, will be committed to completing the work by a certain time. During that period, or while revisions are being carried out by the author on an entire manuscript, the editor must fulfill an elaborate "blue-sheeting" task, in which specific figures are obtained from production and sales regarding every aspect of the book's costs and likely earnings. More elaborate than the preliminary manufacturing estimate, blue-sheeting takes into consideration the specific royalties to be awarded to author and artist, if any are forthcoming; the production costs of the book in different trim sizes; its warehousing costs; and the division's overhead, including payments to the marketing department to cover promotional and other costs. Special formulas based on computerized marketing data are used to project sales at different prices. Final decisions are then made about the price of the book, its size and length, and the number of colors to be used in any illustrations.

If the book is to have illustrations, extra time will be consumed in deciding upon what one editor called "the perfect artist," a task carried out by the editor, usually in consultation with the author; waiting for and accepting or rejecting the sketches and dummies; and separating the completed artwork. Even if a book will not be illustrated, an artist is usually still necessary for the jacket. Decisions must also be made by the editor (and artist, if the work is a picture book), in conjunction with the production manager and staff designer, about the nature and size of the typography to be used in the book; about the number of type lines to a page; about the use of pagination; and about the front matter, frontispiece, and chapter opening designs. Concurrently, the completed manuscript will go through its final examination by the editor, who must forward it to a copy editor for stylistic corrections. At some point in this schedule, the editor must also find time to write the promotional copy for the jacket flaps.

When the manuscript and artwork are completed, the actual manufacturing process can begin. Here, too, the editor watches over the progress of the work—from the correctness of the galleys to the insertion of jackets upon the bound books.

Without an appropriate frame of reference, it is difficult, perhaps, to evaluate the extent of individualized attention to every title's selection and production encouraged by the R&A procedure in response to the client relationship. This frame of reference will be presented, and the differences clearly brought out, through a comparison of the R&A book selection procedure with its mass market counterpart in the first chapter of part 2. The preceding paragraphs have shown, however, that R&A personnel saw the selection process as encouraging the production of artistic creations, of books that conform to the perceived requirements and opportunities of the client relationship. The next section will show how the desire to carry out the mandate of that relationship shapes the editors' specific comments about selecting content.

THE CLIENT RELATIONSHIP AND SELECTION GUIDELINES

R&A's direct selectors had some difficulty responding to questions regarding particular content characteristics. In fact, two key respondents—the publisher and a senior editor—were quite exasperated by the numerous queries along these lines. The publisher spoke for both when, after insisting that her division does not have any formal criteria for book selection, exclaimed: "We just choose good books. If it's a good book, we'll do it."

This insistence that the direct selectors perform their work without any formal guidelines can, in itself, be seen as a reflection of the client relationship, since admitting to specific guidelines might be construed as taking a formulaic approach to what the interviewed subjects liked to portray as an artistic endeavor. Despite their general denial of formal guidelines, however, the publisher, other editors, a reader, the production director, and the finance director did articulate certain policies, general rules, and criteria for dealing with the literary and economic considerations of the book selection and publication process.

Two broad directions regarding selection were particularly evident in the selectors' comments: (1) A commitment, mitigated only under special circumstances, to the primary importance of literary, artistic, aesthetic qualities in the selection characteristics; and (2) a notion, not articulated very often or very explicitly, that the nature, extent, and complexity of the artistic endeavor should vary with the expected age of the reader, according to some general conceptions of childhood and childhood interests. Since it is already clear that these general markers have been shaped by the selectors' conceptualizations of the demands and opportunities of their major client relationship, the more specific guidelines selectors use will now be discussed.

Seasonal Lists

Every year R&A formulates lists, previously mentioned, that represent the total number of new titles that the division will publish during the year. These lists are timed to coincide with the two traditional book publishing seasons, fall and spring; the titles on the lists are released over the months of those seasons. A few editors mentioned in regard to the number of books on the seasonal lists that a triennial assessment of the firm's economic situation, the economic situation of the marketplace, and the firm's strength within the marketplace has produced a guideline that approximately 25–30 books per list should be produced under current conditions. All the interviewed people stressed, however, that because their book selection procedure is based on the notion that in-house conceptualizing of titles is not conducive to the production of good books, and since the editors must rely on the manuscripts authors send in, they are unable to dictate the exact number of publishable manuscripts that should arrive in time to be placed on a particular list.

The recognition of this necessary flexibility and slight relinquishing of control, seen in regard to the number of books on a seasonal list (and one that was traced to the client relationship), was also observed in regard to the types of books that make up a list. One associate editor, responding to a question about her guidelines regarding the relative number of "fantasy" and "reality" books, said:

> We just do the books that look good. It would be nice—wonderful—to
> have on each list a wonderful design of this [content category] and that.
> But you rarely can control it. Authors work at their own pace and you
> can't plug them in and say "you do a fantasy." You just can't.

While two of the editors steadfastly maintained that they have no requirements regarding the division's new book lists, three others and the reader
did point out some general guidelines that editors try to follow in selecting
books for the lists. Two words repeatedly used by the subjects to characterize these guidelines were variety and balance. Both terms refer to the idea
that many titles belonging to a particular category of books are ill-advised
for one season's list. The editors said they try to avoid selecting too many
manuscripts that would lead to such an imbalance.

A primary reason for the varied assortment of new books is the feeling
that librarians might be loath to buy several books on the same topic or
directed at the same age group from one company's list. The editors also
articulated the belief that, since the editors know that librarians have to
serve different age groups and interests, the division should try to parallel
these interests, at least in terms of broad categories, in the hope that librarians will need all the books on the list.

Balancing the List. The R&A selectors' emphasis on the idea of a balanced list centered on the areas of age and grade groupings. In fact, the
reader and an associate editor dolefully pointed out the difficulty of getting
good manuscripts for children in the middle grades, third through fifth.
They quickly admitted that such groupings, determined by each book's
editor, are only suggestive, with the age indications generally directed at
parents and the grade markings listed to aid librarians. Three respondents
added that an editor's decision to affix particular age and grade groupings
to a title usually derives from some general notions about the vocabulary
and number of pages appropriate for a child at a particular age, as well as
from ideas about the experiences and interests of a child at a particular
stage of life. One rule of thumb regarding the latter concern is that a book
with youthful protagonists will appeal to children of approximately the same
age.

An impetus toward a varied list in terms of grade and age levels, as well
as in terms of subject matter, lies in the different interests of the division's
editors. Of course, the manuscripts that cross an editor's desk are determined to some degree by house authors; by those manuscripts that readers
and their supervisor decide to forward; by the kind of material sent to the
editor because of personal contacts and solicitations made in the course
of meeting with writers, agents, and librarians; and, in the case of an
associate editor, by delegated assignments. However, these factors are

themselves influenced to a great extent by the particular expertise and aesthetic leanings of the person involved.

Although no specific interview questions were designed to explore this area, a few editors touched upon the subject in passing. One associate editor noted that, although she has worked on novels, most of the titles she edits are picture books, because that is her best area. Another associate editor stated that while she does not have any particular preference with respect to fiction or nonfiction, most of the editors in the division are fiction-oriented, some preferring to work on books for younger children while others enjoy novels directed at older juveniles. This range of predilections usually ensures that the seasonal lists will include a variety of age and grade groupings, at least in fiction.

As previously noted, R&A has a heritage of fiction, and the division as a whole has continued in this path, assured that the marketplace allows it. However, as implied in the associate editor's comments, not all of the editors in the division are inclined towards fiction. One editor is considered the house's science expert, and, according to the associate editor, a feeling "by the editors" that the division should publish more nonfiction led to the hiring of an editor with predominantly historical interests. Both the science-oriented and history-oriented editors have taken to editing fiction as well, however, and the R&A staff generally denied any requirements or intentions to strictly balance their lists along fiction and nonfiction lines.

The Easy Readers. One clear-cut specification, mentioned by three of the editors in regard to each seasonal list, is that the list should include about two books from the division's easy reader lines—the early easy readers and the regular easy readers. Each of these related lines comprises a group of titles uniform in size, 3-color process, typography, general type layout, number of pages, and price; the last two characteristics define the format differences between early easy readers and easy readers. The easy readers are the only new books on the division's seasonal lists that have a fair sale to bookstores as well as libraries, primarily because of the decisions of some major stores to carry them. The standardization of the easy reader format is the result of the division's attempt to keep the unit costs of the titles at such a level that their trade prices can compete successfully with those of mass market juveniles. A first printing of 25,000 copies, high by library market standards, also helps keep costs down, as does the printing of the small books two at a time on the same printing sheets.

R&A marketing and salespeople, when interviewed, pointed out that the presence of easy readers on the juvenile list sometimes lends an air of commercial attractiveness to the rest of the new books in the eyes of store agents and increases the possibility that they will buy them. In consequence, the editors and readers are constantly seeking manuscripts that will adapt naturally to the easy reader format; they trade notes on potential candidates in and out of editorial meetings. Because the lines are well known, writers sometimes send in manuscripts addressed to those formats. However, the need to sell at least 25,000 copies in first printing tends to narrow the editors' choices to notable library market authors and illustrators.

The somewhat standardized approach to the easy readers, precipitated by an attempt to maintain and extend a foothold in the bookstore market, represents a departure from the division's extremely individualized approach to books. Realizing this, three direct selectors went out of their way to stress the points of compatibility of the easy reader titles with the mandate of the major client relationship. One associate editor, when asked if she has any guidelines regarding vocabulary control, referred proudly to the easy reader lines in the following manner:

> We don't have any guidelines. On the [easy reader] books you can tell. I mean, you [i.e., the editor] have to eliminate four syllable problems and very difficult sentence construction, but you do that after the story is written. You do that as organically as you can—without handing an author a list of words and saying "write a story using those words." That's why the books are artistic. That's why they work as stories, because their impulse is the story, first, with a writer who can naturally write simply and directly.

Guidelines for Good Books

The perceived mandate of the client relationship to produce artistic books was clearly reflected in the direct selectors' responses to questions about their guidelines for the content of the titles they select. Few concrete, positive specifications were forthcoming in response to these questions, since the selectors insisted that they have no formal guidelines and implied that formal guidelines would not be conducive to the production of good books. Nevertheless, their comments about plot, subject matter, style, and characterization reveal their priorities concerning the elements of good books, as well as their confidence in their ability to successfully present their personal likings to clients.

Plot and Subject Matter. All the subjects willingly agreed that the plot of a fiction title is important, but noted that since each book is looked at in individual terms, no specifications can be given regarding this content characteristic. An associate editor echoed her colleagues when she spoke about plot in the following manner:

> A plot has to be successful on the terms that it's trying to be successful. It has to be convincing. It can't be too contrived. It sounds simple, but it's true.

34

Q. Do books have to have a plot?

A. No. We have plotless books. We have books that have a thread of emotion that binds them together. Picture books especially. [An editor's own] books, especially. It just has to have an overall design to it. It doesn't have to have a literal value.

Q. Does it have to have action?

A. If it keeps our interest, it has action. Some books have emotional action rather than plot action.

When asked about subject matter, the R&A editors, reflecting an admitted bias, spoke about fiction. They agreed that the particular subject is really not important; the handling of the subject is what really counts. The same associate editor stated:

As long as it [the subject] is honest, straightforward, and done artistically. My books are on every theme and subject.

Q. Is there anything you're looking for?

A. No.

Q. Anything too overdone?

A. No. There's no taboo. Even if a book has been overdone. If it's done well, then it can be done again.

The other associate editor, while concurring with her colleague, emphasized that she follows two fundamental criteria in gauging the acceptability of a manuscript; the interest it holds for her ("If I'm bored, a child will be bored"), and her conception of the abilities of children who will read the book. With regard to the latter, she stated that an editor must insure that a manuscript's subject is within the realm of experience of the age group indicated by the prospective book's vocabulary and format.

Style and Characterization. The connection made by the first associate editor between the acceptability of subject matter and its execution was particularly stressed by the selectors when they were asked about their guidelines regarding style. All the subjects agreed that a personal style complementary to the story is important. No preference was voiced for poetry or prose, though two participants did note that good poetry for children is hard to find. Interestingly, one of the editors referred to a "series," a book form that combines subject and style, as a format generally of unacceptable quality for her division. "Our books do not follow formula-type ideas like 'Nancy Drew' or 'The Hardy Boys,' " she stressed.

The importance of individual, nonformulaic style and approach could also be seen in the comments regarding characterization. The need for the convincing, nonexploitive delineation of protagonists was generally stressed, with one editor adding that the characters have to be of a type that "children respond to." A primary literary-aesthetic orientation towards characterization was seen in the remarks of all the subjects, and is embodied in the following remarks by an associate editor:

> The same standards of judgment apply that apply to adult fiction. Quality of writing. Strength of development. Honesty and believability of portrayal. This is absolutely true from the lowest to the highest ages. We generally look for characterization over plot. I suppose this is true for good literature in general. The important thing is that the story comes out and reveals the character.

The primary emphasis on the literary, artistic nature of characterization is also evident in the comments by the reader and the two interviewed senior editors on the racial and sexual mix of their books and in their responses to a question regarding guidelines on the division of their seasonal lists into books for general audiences, as contrasted with books for particular racial and/or ethnic groups. All the direct selectors denied any guidelines, the reader saying that, while such books are actively sought, the selectors

> ... try not to make that a primary factor, because you start thinking less in terms of quality and more in didactic terms, which is fine except that generally it means you're publishing inferior fiction. Which is not even going to fulfill a good social purpose.

The selectors also denied the use of guidelines when questioned about the appearance of racial characters as minor figures in books; an associate editor noted that "blacks and Third World people" were added in some cases "if they fall naturally into a book," and that editors have suggested that artists include more minority representatives in the illustrations. That same individual also pointed out that she and her colleagues "try to inform an author if he's doing something sexist. We don't force him to make any changes he doesn't want to make. We just try to see if he's giving a 'roundedness' in his portrayals."

Another area of characterization lacking formal guidelines involved the use of animals or people as central characters. Two participants—the reader and an editor—did admit to a wariness concerning anthropomorphic portrayals. Regarding such characterization, the reader noted that there is "a fine line between making it good and making it horrible. We do get terrible manuscripts, like 'Patsy Paper Plate'—a plate that comes to life and bemoans her fate as a paper plate. I mean, we get a lot of garbage. It's easy to write garbage."

The Moral Point of View

That the client relationship causes publishers to be concerned primarily with the literary quality of a manuscript and the artistic vision of its author also influenced the selector's remarks regarding the moral point of view of the works they publish. One prominent manifestation of this influence was a denial of any intention to inculcate morality. The following comments of an associate editor are representative in this regard:

> We don't look for a moral. We look for a story that has meaning. Any story that's well-written has a statement somewhere in it, but we don't look for stories that are written to have a statement. We look for literary works. Period.

The publisher and the two senior editors hinted at some of the tensions that exist between the desire to publish innovative books that reflect an artist's unique style, and the recognition that some ethical lines should not, perhaps, be crossed. One editor commented that the question regarding a moral point of view was very ambiguous and difficult to answer briefly. The publisher managed to state the collective viewpoint concisely:

> We feel that a book should be a reflection of the author's own consistent morality. Beyond that, it's a very difficult question to answer. Certainly, if the book is evil we won't publish it, no matter what its literary merits.

The division's reader, emphasizing the special importance of a moral point of view in the case of juvenile books, elaborated on the tensions that this aspect of content can create:

> [A moral point of view] is important, particularly since you're dealing with kids. And it's not always easy. I mean, that's the hardest thing. If a book is beautifully written and you think that the author's mind and values are disturbed, that can be tough. A few times we've published books that I've felt violently opposed to the ethics. But, obviously, the editor and the head of the department who passed judgment upon it didn't agree, because we'd never publish anything that we thought was perverted because we thought it might sell or was dazzling writing. Sometimes it's hard to know. Sometimes that can happen even in the younger area, where the portrayal of a relationship between a mother and a child might cause one person to think "Gee, this is really sick," and another person might think "This is really charming."

Although the direct selectors did reveal some self-doubt and conflict regarding the moral point of view in some manuscripts they select, they exhibited confidence on the subject of controversial issues. The subjects pointed out that since the 1960s, few areas of life have not been dealt with in children's literature. Drugs, abortion, racial discrimination, gang warfare, and homosexuality—these and other controversial subjects have been dealt with in R&A books.

Replying to a question about controversial issues that had affected her work during the past year, the publisher contended that no issue is too controversial for editorial selection: "I don't think there should be any taboos, if handled properly." While she did not elaborate on what such proper handling entails, her remarks regarding a moral point of view and comments by other R&A editors did indicate that the books dealing with sensitive personal and societal problems are expected to contain some positive moral uplift, although they need not, and often do not, contain happy endings. In actuality, the selectors raised only one issue that had consistently drawn a great deal of recent protest—curse words. Two editors and the promotion director noted that such protests have not deterred the use of four-letter words where applicable, since, in the words of one participant, "if it's true to the spirit of the book, it has its place."

The confidence of the editors in dealing with these sensitive areas can be traced to an aspect of the client relationship that has not as yet been highlighted—the support that libraries give the publishers by acting as protective buffers between them and complaining community groups. Significantly, it was the promotion director who explained this situation most explicitly:

> I find most librarians so terrific, really. They care, and they're in the forefront, obviously. I can sympathize with what a lot of them put up with from parents around the country. But librarians around the country have, on their own, established guidelines on how to handle such things.

Guidelines for Illustrations and Format

The editors considered illustrations and format very important to the creation of a successful title, particularly in a picture book. However, these content characteristics were not discussed simultaneously with writing style, plot, subject matter, and characterization, because an additional aspect relating to the client relationship could be seen to influence these two non-written elements—cost.

Illustrations and Cover Art. As in the case of the other content characteristics, the direct selectors contended that no specific guidelines could be presented for illustrations or cover art, since the choice of both the artist and the illustrations depend on the nature of the individual manuscript under consideration. Certain kinds of work were, however, deemed unacceptable by R&A personnel. One editor pointed out that while a book's cover art should be impressionable, "so that when you look at it, you feel you want to open the book," it should not be as arresting as mass market paperback covers, which "flash things up" and are "as noisy as possible." The reader and an editor disparaged "cartoonish" illustrations as cheap and not artistic, while all the respondents noted that the division has not followed a prominent library market trend to incorporate near-abstract art into picture books. The editors agreed that such illustrations "lack meaning for children" and represent "art for arty's sake."

While the interviewed subjects' remarks on selection represent their quite consistent aesthetic interpretation of the perceived mandate from the client relationship to produce good books, other major decisions regarding artwork—the use of color and the selection of artists—are intimately connected to economic, not aesthetic, judgments about the firm and its marketplace. A key factor is the cost of color illustration. The assistant production director pointed out that there is a substantial difference in cost between a 3-color and a 4-color book. Moreover, while the division can sell approximately 8,000 copies of a title illustrated in black-and-white, or 10,000 copies of a 3-color picture book at an acceptable library market price and still have a chance to break even or make a profit, the 4-color process that R&A uses, in which the colors are separated by camera rather than by hand, has mandated a printing of about 25,000 if the book is to be realistically sold for below $8, the division's limit for all but extremely unusual books.

The required first printing of at least 25,000 copies of a 4-color picture book has, as in the case of the 3-color easy readers, dictated a situation whereby only extremely popular authors and illustrators (or author-illustrators), whose sales can be reliably predicted at the 25,000 level, will be used. The production director noted that the division has been doing fewer and fewer 4-color books each year because of the difficulty of meeting that criterion in the crowded and highly competitive library market. She and the other direct selectors were quick to emphasize, however, that librarians have shown a great appreciation for 3-color and even black-and-white picture books, and that evidently children like them, too.

Format. Rising costs were also seen as having consequences for the size and length of the division's books. Several respondents pointed to the movement throughout the library market segment towards standardized trim sizes and folio lengths, a result of rising manufacturing costs and diminished library funds in the 1970s. The assistant production director noted that the division is currently trying to fit its books into seven trim sizes; the seven sizes are most economical because, during printing, the pages cover the entire printing sheet and leave no wasted space. Unusual sizes and shapes are sometimes produced, but only in cases of author-illustrators who are popular in the library market, where a large first printing is justified. In general, the higher the anticipated sales and the lower the unit costs, the more idiosyncratic a book can be in terms of size, length, and paper type.

One area of overall design that direct selectors contended still has no budget-related guidelines surrounding it is typography. They said that R&A's designer, in consultation with the editor, has free reign in choosing the most aesthetically appropriate typeface to use. A few respondents noted, however, that the typeface must be big enough for children of the anticipated age group to want to read it. Certain measurements, designated by points, have become accepted for certain ages. For example, easy readers have 18 point type, regular picture books tend to have typefaces of 14 points, and books for older children might be printed in a 12 or 11 point typeface. With all books except the easy readers, however, points are not standard, since design variations among various typefaces might cause one face to actually be smaller or larger than another with the same point value.

While the choice of typography is relatively unspecified, the choice of bindings is completely determined. R&A designates three types of bindings for its titles: two trade bindings, placed on the small number of new books sold to bookstores (with titles having 32 or fewer pages getting one kind and those having more than 32 pages getting the other), and a library binding. All three bindings are sewn, though the techniques used in library bindings, side sewing, is more durable and expensive than the saddle stitched or smythe-sewn bindings on trade editions. The assistant production director explained that library bindings are produced in response to librarians' willingness to pay more than store personnel for a book that will stand up to high circulation and wear.

The R&A selectors' assessments of economic and aesthetic requirements, preferences, and leverages on their side of the client relationship and on the outlet side have been observed to shape their guidelines with regard to both the frequency and diversity of certain types of illustrations and formats. To see if the influence of the client relationship extends to the actual books the division publishes, a brief analysis was made of the new titles R&A produced during the 1974 spring and 1975 fall seasons. The difference in output for the two seasons, 28 for the fall, 19 for the spring, supports the respondents' claim that, within limits, their list size depends on the number of good books they can find to publish in a particular season. As predicted, the focus of the list was on fiction, the division's self-professed forte. The need for easy readers and the particular preference of two editors for picture books was reflected in those titles' accounting for 40 percent of the division's output. Titles aimed predominantly at children over 10 years old made up the highest percentage among age categories, however, with titles for the 6 to 10 year set—a group an editor admitted is difficult to find good books for—being lowest in representation. Fantasy, a subject editors noted as problematic, was also low in representation; only one fantasy was released among the 47 titles.

Regarding characterization, the list contained an interesting absence of anthropomorphic portrayals, a fairly equal representation of males and females as main characters, and one title—a biography—about a black man. The format and price categories also generally reflected the considerations and guidelines that the selectors noted. Only 2 books were produced in 4 colors, while 26 titles presented 3-color and 2-color illustrations. Another corroboration of the interviews is that the books were priced below $8, with the great majority around $5 and $6. However, two findings regarding format did not conform to expectations. Contrary to the assistant production director's statement that the firm is trying to hold the number of trim sizes to seven, fifteen different sizes were found on the lists. Another discrepancy is that no easy readers were placed on the spring list, contrary to the editors' noting a need for about 2 per season. One explanation might be that this specification regarding the easy readers, which are marketable to bookstores, really applies only to the fall, when the commercial outlets tend to increase their stock in anticipation of Christmas shopping.

THE CLIENT RELATIONSHIP AND
THE ULTIMATE AUDIENCE

Despite the minor inconsistencies just mentioned, the influence of the library market client relationship has been seen to extend beyond the guidelines of R&A personnel to the actual books produced during two seasons. One area that has not received enough attention from the standpoint of the client relationship, however, is the image held by the selectors of their purported ultimate audience, children. Actually, the selectors' implicit image of that audience has already been shown to be a consequence of their feedback from librarians, coupled with their generalized conceptions of children and their recognition that balancing seasonal lists by age will make the list more attractive to librarians, causing them to buy all the titles. This final section will examine the more explicit images held by the editors and reader of their audience.

In reply to the audience-related question on the interview schedule—"What image do you have of the people who read your books?"—all of the editors either implied or admitted that they simply do not think in such terms. The publisher stated concisely that "we don't have an image. Every author writes for the child inside himself." One of the editors echoed the publisher on this score but added the opinion that children who visit the library still get "what they really want," since librarians choose the books they feel children will like. When asked whether she feels mass market or library market books come closest to giving children what they really want, she opined that library market titles fulfill juvenile desires best, since in libraries children can choose their books and thereby communicate their true likes and dislikes to the librarians, while in bookstores parents who "don't know what they're buying" often purchase books without consulting their youngsters.

While two of the respondents were categorical in denying the espousal of an audience image, three did suggest some characteristics of their ultimate readers. An editor, after indicating that she really has no information about her audience, speculated that "I suppose we reach all kinds of children. A multifaceted audience, you might say." An associate editor was more expansive in her reply:

> I have no image. They're the great invisible face out there. No, we don't have an image.
> Q. How did you arrive at that image?
> A. By ignorance. [laughing] There are certain books you know will appeal to kids who don't read as well as do other kids. And there are certain books that you know have more sophisticated ideas, who have introspective heroines, and you know the average kid isn't going to read all those books. But they are quite vague little notions. They're not rigidly defined.

This associate editor's tendency, towards the end of her response, to infer the nature of her audience from the nature of the books that the division publishes can be seen in an even more pronounced form in these remarks by R&A's reader:

> I think readers of our books tend to be not necessarily the average child. Probably pretty good readers. We try not to be too overweighted on this side because you don't want to be publishing books for little rarefied prima donnas, but a lot of our books *are* more sensitive or quiet. Books for the unusual child.
> Q. How did you arrive at that image?
> A. Well, it's just that we go for books that conform to high literary standards and a lot of emotional depth. And those are not going to be runaway bestsellers with all kids. We try not to be too fastidious and demanding, because children have a right to light fiction as much as adults. And good, well-written nonfiction. Not everything serious.

Clearly, when the direct selectors have an image of the people who read their books, it is one that merely reflects their views on the types of books they publish. The "probably pretty good readers" mentioned by R&A's reader are a reflection of her realization that the division's selectors "go for high literary standards and a lot of emotional depth." However, the reader's remarks, and those of an editor and associate editor, also implied different types and sizes of audiences with different literary interests. This notion of a multifaceted audience is a reflection of the varied—though literarily and aesthetically inclined—list that editors feel they should create. Extentionally, then, the selectors' audience image can be said to reflect their understanding of the demands and possibilities in R&A's major client relationship.

This chapter illustrates how the library market client relationship exerts a systemic influence upon one important publishing firm's juvenile book selection and production process. R&A selectors interpret feedback from throughout the children's book complex with an eye on their division's major distribution outlets—libraries. The selectors' approach to such problems as rising printing costs, material costs, and anger over the use of curse words results from evaluating requirements, preferences, and leverages on their side and on the patron side of the client relationship. In short, this chapter has delineated the crucial consequences that continual producer-patron interactions bring about for an important producer. Do such interactions also exert strong influence on the activities of an important patron? The next chapter will take up this question.

Chapter 3: The Library Market
Distribution Outlet

Metrosystem, the library to be examined in this chapter, is located in an ethnically diverse urban center that contains more than one million people. The system has two major book-buying and distributing arms oriented toward different audiences—the Adult/Young Adult Division and the Children's Division. The entire library has about three million volumes in stock, with little less than a million of those belonging to the children's division. In recent years that division has been transacting about one and a half million book loans a year.

The Children's Division and the Adult/Young Adult Division share space in the library's 50 sections, including 46 branches, a bookmobile service, a service that deposits books in schools with no libraries and lends books to the handicapped, a regional branch, and a central branch. The branches are meant to serve specific neighborhoods within the city; the two special service areas are designed to make the library more accessible to children and adults who cannot use it easily; and the regional library is equipped to serve the broad and specialized needs of a large district far from the central branch. These sections are overseen by each division's nerve center— its System Coordinating Office. The purpose of both coordinating offices is to direct divisional planning and policy; to coordinate the selection, processing, and purchasing of books, records, and filmstrips; and to initiate and carry out various entertainment programs for their audiences throughout the year.

The head of the Children's System Coordinating Office controls the entire range of children's division activities, many of which go beyond the book selection domain that is this chapter's concern. Although she is ultimately responsible to the director and associate director of the entire library system (which supports an Adult/Young Adult Division as its other major book-buying unit), the head of the coordinating office is a nationally known figure who has been at her position for over a decade and, at the admission of the director, has autonomy in creating policies within the juvenile division.

The head of the System Coordinating Office delegates much of the day to day responsibility of the book, record, and film selection process to her head of book selection who, in turn, has two coordinators of lower rank to help her, one for book and the other for nonbook materials. The regional library's area coordinator also has an active role in the selection of books, particularly in the regional library and the branches surrounding it. The coordinators are former branch librarians who took special civil service tests to work in the coordinating office and to advance to one of three levels there.

Branch librarianship also has three levels. Beginners (who must have a master's degree in Library Science) start at Level 1 and may advance by taking (and excelling on) competitive exams to become assistant branch head (Level 2) or branch head (Level 3) when an appropriate position is vacant. It should be noted that not every branch has a children's librarian. Insufficient funding and the necessity to staff the central branch with two librarians has set the number of sections with children's librarians to 44 (out of 50) and the number of individuals in such positions to 45. In view of the Preface's discussion of the traditional female domination of this profession, it should not be too surprising that all the coordinators and children's librarians are women.

This chapter will examine the activities of these librarians with the aim of describing the consequences of their interaction with major suppliers upon their selection of books for Metrosystem's branches. The client relationship has already been shown to influence the entire structure and operation of the library market children's publishing division of R&A Publishing. The following discussion of Metrosystem's book selection will show that the relationship influences the distribution outlet as well: it functions to ensure that the output of library market suppliers like R&A will remain the primary preference of Metrosystem's selectors, and it helps perpetuate the power of already dominant firms to set trends and define issues.

THE BOOK SELECTION PROCEDURE

The impact of the client relationship upon Metrosystem is not as all-encompassing as it is in R&A. The fundamental selection goals of the library stem not from the client relationship but, rather, from the organization's position as a publicly funded entity ultimately responsible to city and state officials. Nevertheless, the librarians' answers to interview and survey questions reveal that the client relationship influences their particular selection guidelines and, consequently, the types of books they accept and reject, the titles they single out for special attention, and the innovations they are willing to introduce.

Not surprisingly, the most direct influence of the client relationship can be noted among those librarians continually in contact with representatives from publishing firms, the coordinators. Since it is this group that sets children's library policy and ensures that the branch librarians are guided by that policy, it is significant that the interaction with major suppliers has most effect on them. Yet, as will be seen, the unequal influence of this interaction on coordinators and branch librarians does cause some tension between the two groups and lessens the power of the client relationship somewhat.

The approaches of the coordinators and branch librarians to their client relationship and the consequences of those approaches for book selection can be noted most specifically by examining two broad considerations that shape the selection procedure: the perception of general requirements regarding selection material and the manner in which such material is introduced to the organization.

GENERAL SELECTION REQUIREMENTS

Sara Fenwick, in reviewing the history of library service to children, notes that from the start "all such efforts were directed quite consistently toward a goal of providing books for youth that would foster their education as effective and useful citizens. With a variety of interpretations and in many different settings, this goal has continued throughout the past 150 years."[1] Interestingly, her comments apply quite well to the Metrosystem Children's Division. Consider the following "General Statement of Objectives" in the System Coordinating Office's policy handbook for new librarians:

> The library's primary objective is to develop in children an enjoyment and appreciation of reading for "reading's sake" and to provide books of literary quality as well as other material (film, records, etc.) which will satisfy a child's recreational needs and natural curiosity, thus contributing to his growth as an intelligent world citizen.

This quote, recalled by the coordinators and by a few branch librarians, was quite compatible with the answers all those interviewed gave when asked about their goals. As written, the passage might be said to represent a public interest stance, a perspective that links the requirement of literary quality to a concern with the emotional growth of readers, their adjustment and social integration. Note, however, that while the subjects did not contradict each other or the general statement when enunciating their goals, they did differ in their relative emphasis on literary quality and enjoyment as the primary selection requirement. Moreover, the coordinators and branch librarians differed along these lines, with the former group emphasizing high literary quality and the latter group stressing the importance of a book's potential enjoyment and, more particularly, its popularity. An example of this variance is found in the following statements by the head of the coordinating office and a branch librarian, respectively:

> Our objective is to promote communication between the child and thinkers of the world. To present to the child writers and illustrators of quality materials.
> My objective is to introduce children to books; to help them enjoy reading. I work in an inner-city area where the reading level is *extremely* low. I'm particularly interested in reading motivation programs, using storytelling and book talks.

A quantitative indication that popularity is indeed more important to the branch librarians than to the coordinators can be found in the fact that 29 (91%) of the 32 branch librarians who responded to the questionnaire said that general impressions of what children like is very important in their selection of books for their branches. By contrast, the three responding coordinators, who answered questions relating to branch selection in their capacities as book buyers for outlets without children's librarians, all answered that children's preferences are only somewhat important.

Budgetary Considerations

Although compatibility with the noneconomic public interest stance was the preeminent requirement to selectors, budgetary considerations were also noted by them as very important, specifically with regard to choosing titles for the various branches. The amount of money a librarian is given to spend on the purchase of new books could be expected to have an important influence on her book choices. Indeed, 29 (89%) of the questionnaire respondents said it is very important for that purpose. However, from the standpoint of librarians' perceptions of general selection requirements that shape selection guidelines, the importance of the budget lies not in the amount of money doled to particular librarians. Rather, the budget's importance lies in the manner in which that money is allocated.

Approximately 30 percent of the money apportioned by the head of book selection to the branches for book-buying is distributed evenly among the branches; another 30 percent is divided in direct proportion to each branch's book circulation figures; and about 40 percent is doled by the head of the System Coordinating Office and the head of book selection at their discretion. Both coordinators, in their interviews, tended to downplay the importance of circulation for a branch's monetary allotment and stressed that the discretionary cash is often used to provide extra funds to chronically low circulation branches so that they might improve their collections.

Some branch librarians, however, were not so sanguine about their chances of maintaining or increasing their budgets without maintaining or increasing their circulation statistics. Of the 35 survey questionnaire respondents, 8 (23%) said that current circulation figures are very important considerations when they select books for their branches; 14 (40%) described this information as somewhat important; 11 answered not important; and 2 had no opinion. One coordinator gave the impression that concern over circulation is more widespread than these numbers indicate when she opined that "everyone [i.e., every branch librarian] is under pressure to a certain extent to keep circulation up." This pressure was translated into a book selection requirement among the four branch librarians who emphasized it; they viewed the allocation of funds according to circulation as a mandate to consider only the minimum standards of literary quality in their search for books that show promise of a quick turnover.

However, a desire to maintain or increase circulation was not the only reason for the branch librarians' lesser emphasis than the coordinators on high literary quality in their articulation of selection requirements. When asked whether they would buy more quality books for small potential audiences if they did not have to report circulation statistics but did have their current book-buying budgets, 23 (72%) of the 32 branch librarian respondents to the survey questionnaire said "no," while only 7 (22%) said "yes"; 3 were "not sure." The high percentage of negative answers would seem to indicate that another factor, perhaps more important than the perceived need to increase circulation, is impelling the branch librarians toward popularity.

Interaction with Children

The other factor that seems to be at the root of the lesser emphasis by the branch librarians on high literary quality and greater emphasis on popularity, as compared to the coordinators, is their close, continual interaction with children, an interaction which the coordinating office librarians, because of the administrative nature of their positions, do not enjoy.[2] Several branch librarians, in interviews or informal discussions, noted that working on the floor, listening to children's requests, helping students with school assignments, and dealing firsthand with the low reading abilities of many of them, yields a perspective that shifts the foremost emphasis of book selection from quality to popularity. One long-time librarian echoed many of her branch colleagues when she noted that the coordinators "don't get out [on the branch floors] that much. So there is sometimes a gap in what the librarians on the floor perceive and what they [i.e., the coordinators] think is going on. I think there is a tremendous gap sometimes."

The Client Relationship

The difference between the coordinators and branch librarians on the subject of literary quality was reinforced through the former group's differential contact with those extraorganizational activities noted by the focal library market publishing selectors, activities used by firms to influence the librarians' perceptions of good books. Data from the questionnaire survey supports interview findings that while all the coordinators frequently attend library conferences, are often in contact with editors and other publishers' representatives, and know quite a bit about current happenings within the children's book industry, the majority of branch librarians rarely go to conferences, speak to publishing selectors, or know very much about the industry or its imprints.

All of the branch personnel did, however, recognize the strong connections between the coordinators, particularly the head of the System Coordinating Office, and the major book producers. The head of book selection characterized the relationship in the following manner:

> [The links are] very strong. Because [the head of the coordinating office] is very prominent and has been working with children's books for a long time and is respected highly. So she really knows book publishers—the ones who've left and the ones who are there now. And she does a lot of work through the American Library Association which involves promoting books in general and *publishers whom she likes* [italics added].
>
> Q. What about your interactions with publishers' representatives?
> A. I don't get to know all of them. I'll meet someone, say, at an American Library Association meeting. I'm a representative of the liaison committee with the Children's Book Council, which is half librarians and half children's book editors and promoters.
> Q. So there is a lot of interaction?
> A. A fair amount.

The head of the coordinating office pointed out that she is well aware of promotional tactics that impinge upon her and her associates during these and other interactions with publishers' representatives. She contended, however, that such influences are two-way; that by allowing publishers to ask favors of her, such as the review of manuscripts and promotion of books through her, she receives the opportunity to make a mark on their selection activities.

The chief coordinator also noted that some promotional operations are valuable from the standpoint of her own library system. Invitations to sales conferences, she said, give her advance knowledge about books, knowledge useful for evaluating titles on similar subjects already being considered by Metrosystem librarians for selection. If she feels that the previewed book is better, she will state her views within Metrosystem in the hope that the selectors will wait for the superior title.

Even such an obvious promotional practice on the part of publishers as an author's or illustrator's visit to the library system was seen by the chief coordinator as a vehicle to selectively spotlight those "thinkers of the world" whom she would like her branch librarians to favor in their book-buying and presentations to children. She understood quite clearly that she and her office act as promotional agents for the publishers in this activity. Far from feeling defensive or used, however, the head of the coordinating office welcomed the opportunity and power to promote those who are producing quality literature. She pointed out that it is through the recognition and purchase of books by such authors that Metrosystem has achieved its reputation as a repository of quality children's literature, a reputation that, she and the other coordinators stressed, is important to maintain.

Need to Maintain Quality. The importance of cultivating Metrosystem's reputation for a quality collection can, interestingly enough, be traced to the client relationship—specifically to the coordinators' desires to be influential in that relationship. Two of them suggested that the knowledge that a large library system, such as Metrosystem, will purchase quality titles might assure children's publishers interested in producing such books that their output is likely to find an influential outlet. Also, the influence of the coordinators in promoting the cause of quality books to publishers is likely to be stronger, and their positions more credible, if it is known that the system they oversee emphasizes books that are esteemed by publishers, review media, and other influential librarians.

The coordinators maintain the quality image of the Metrosystem collection by turning to the library market environment, both to ensure that they are actually choosing quality and to participate in defining the term. The first purpose underlies the coordinators' use of review media for comparison with their own critiques. Although titles are often considered for acceptance at the System Coordinating Office before any published reviews appear, all rejected books are held for a year in order to gauge the general critical reaction. While both coordinators and branch librarians indicated that they often disagree with reviews regarding acceptance or rejection, the four coordinators who were interviewed gave examples of cases where favorable consensus on the part of important media had brought them to change their verdicts from negative to positive. "We make mistakes," said the assistant to the head of book selection, adding that Metrosystem is an important library system and should have all the important children's books in the collection.

In defining quality, the System Coordinating Office participates with one of the city's library schools in organizing programs and conferences around themes in children's literature. Drawing attention to quality materials is also the purpose of various book lists that the coordinating office, with the help of branch librarians, assembles and releases to the Metrosystem branches, to other library systems, and to publishing firms. Perhaps the most important list, in terms of publicity and impact, is the annual review of the best new books. Compiled by the chief coordinator and the head of book selection, the chief central branch librarian, and the regional area coordinator, these approximately 100 titles are exhibited and described each spring to an audience of about 300 to 400 people, mostly the city's school librarians, publishers' representatives, and librarians from other municipalities, although nonprofessionals are invited and some do come.

Commitment to Quality. It should, perhaps, be stressed that while the coordinators were seen to differ from the branch personnel in their primary emphasis on quality, rather than popularity, the difference between the attitudes of the two groups was a matter of degree, not kind. The branch librarians showed their commitment to the literary-aesthetic aspect of children's books in their interviews and questionnaire responses. Regarding the latter, 14 (44%) of the 32 branch librarians who were asked about the "extent to which the book [under consideration] is of very high quality" has importance for them when choosing books for their branches, agreed with the coordinators that it is very important; 16 (50%) said it is somewhat important, and only 1 person said that it is not important at all. While the strength of attachment to this area was, in many cases, superseded by an articulated desire to give children "what they like to read" (which, as noted, 91% thought very important), it was, nevertheless, seen to be rather strong.

Evidence that the branch librarians have a lower limit regarding acceptance that is based on conceptions of quality can also be seen in the unanimously negative response that all the interviewed subjects gave when asked if they would buy mass market books for Metrosystem. (A question on the interview schedule defined mass market books as those which are most commonly found in book, department, chain, and variety stores.) Even the seven respondents who had explicitly decried what they saw as the coordinating office's overemphasis on quality at the expense of popularity—and who, it will be seen, did covet some mass market titles that the coordinators had barred—were repelled by the idea of indiscriminately opening the doors to this class of books, regardless of its potential popularity. The following justification is representative:

> I don't think they [i.e., mass market books] are as good as our books. Otherwise we'd be buying them. But I think that anything that will get a child to read in the home—yes, let them use it. . . . A child can read all these books which we don't buy. Fine. But once he gets into the library, he can realize that there is something *more*, that is just as interesting. All you have to do is convince him of that. All you have to do is get a good librarian between the book and the child.

The branch librarians' perspective on the importance of and the guidelines for literary quality were apparently shaped by two major, complementary influences. The relevance of library school training was spontaneously noted by a few; though it was considered very important for branch book selection by only 7 (20%) of the survey respondents, 19 others (57%) thought it somewhat important. Remarks by most subjects showed a continual reinforcement of the literary quality orientation of library school by the System Coordinating Office through periodic reminders by the coordinators in the promotional activities mentioned earler, in bimonthly talks to the entire staff, in personal interactions, and through rotating service on the book selection committee which emphasizes quality. A few branch librarians and all the coordinators noted that a pragmatic incentive for buying titles of high literary quality is found in the coordinators' annual inspection of every branch and scrutiny of all large book replacement orders, with the purpose of maintaining control over. the reputation of the overall collection.[3]

HOW MATERIAL IS INTRODUCED

The preceding has indicated how the influence of the library market client relationship serves to reinforce the emphasis on high literary quality among the coordinating office's librarians and to encourage them to transmit the marketplace's current definitions of quality to their branch personnel. Remarks by all interviewed Metrosystem librarians showed that the dominance of the library market client relationship, as well as the approach to books it shapes, is also reinforced through the manner in which books are introduced to the organization.

The practice used by almost all children's book publishing firms, that of sending review copies to large library systems with the tacit understanding that the books will be reviewed with regard to acceptance or rejection, is one promotional activity mentioned by all the interviewed coordinators. Many major firms, including R&A, offer a contract plan, in which new children's titles are shipped to a library at one-third their regular cost. Metrosystem subscribes to most of these plans; this activity, together with incidental review copies from other firms, inundates the coordinating office with new books every month.

Aside from fulfilling the obvious purpose of getting librarians to recognize the availability of particular titles, the publishers' review copy activity has the cumulative effect of reinforcing among librarians the need to make decisions on the acceptability of a book's content after reading it (or careful reviews of it), and not simply after superficially judging the title by author, publisher, and general subject. The literary quality or good books perspective consequently cultivated in Metrosystem reinforces the influence of publishers who adopt that perspective. Interestingly, because of its silent message about the importance of an individual title's content, the review copy activity also increases the chances that a new publisher with a very small list will find acceptance. In this respect, the review copy promotional activity actually weakens the dominance of large library market juvenile divisions and serves as a counterbalance to what a long-time professional observer of the juvenile book industry has called the "incestuous" relationship between key library coordinators, review media personnel, and representatives of major publishing firms.

The Book Selection Process

The inundation of the System Coordinating Office with new titles, and the consequent inability of any small group of coordinators to critically review all of them, has fostered the routinization of book reviewing and selection through a two-tiered operation. The operation is structured in such a way that the coordinators are in ultimate control, though considerable freedom within usually-agreed-upon acceptance boundaries mitigates the tension between them and branch personnel regarding the differing emphasis of the two groups on literary quality and popularity.

In the first level of book selection, books are examined for general acceptability to the system as a whole. Each month the branch librarians and the coordinators choose or, more rarely, are assigned newly arrived books to review for the next book selection committee meeting, held monthly from September to June.[4] That committee of 11, chaired by the head of book selection and comprised of her two assistants, the regional area coordinator, and an annually rotating panel of branch librarians, decides whether any reviewer's recommendations on system acceptance or rejection of titles, including placing them in the regional and/or central

53

branches or in a special, noncirculating collection, should be contested. If so, the book is often sent out for another review. The majority decision by the committee must be approved by—and can be vetoed by—either the head of book selection or the head of the coordinating office.

After these selection decisions are made, a list is drawn up indicating the final status of each book. Thereupon, the branch librarians come to the coordinating office to decide which of the accepted books they would like to buy for their particular branches. Branches without children's librarians have their books bought for them by coordinating office librarians, the regional area coordinator, or the additional librarian in the central branch. During this branch selection process, the librarians are encouraged to examine the books, as well as to peruse the staff review(s) of each. When all the branch orders are completed at the end of the month, they are sent to the library system's acquisitions department, where they are consolidated and assigned to one or more jobbers. The book selection head estimated that most books end up on branch shelves approximately six months after publication date.

Each level of the two-tiered procedure calls attention to one of the competing primary requirements for selection. The questionnaire survey corroborated as widespread the opinions of several interviewed subjects that their main concern, when reviewing a book for system-level selection, is "the extent to which the book is of very high quality": 23 (72%) of the 32 responding branch librarians thought this factor very important at this stage of reviewing, while only 11 (34%) felt that way about their "general impressions about what [the city's] children want to read." In striking contrast, when asked about branch-level selection, 30 (94%) of the branch personnel felt that their "general impressions about what the children in [their] branch area like to read" is very important, while only 13 (41%) thought the high quality statement rated that designation.

Three librarians who explained these different approaches to books at the branch and system levels pointed out that since reviewers do not have to purchase the books they laud, and since they are not familiar with the capabilities and predilections of children in the many neighborhoods throughout the city, they conform easily to the general reviewing pattern of writing predominantly literary-aesthetic critiques. When it comes to actually purchasing, they said, individual librarians evaluate a reviewer's synopsis of the story and judgment with their particular branches in mind.

Despite their acceptance of the literary quality perspective as the basis for system-level selection, several branch personnel evidenced some annoyance with the coordinators regarding that reviewing tier. Four librarians noted instances in which the head of the coordinating office superseded their unfavorable reviews as well as the Book Selection Committee's concurrence, and accepted titles, allegedly because of her friendship with or personal esteem for an author or illustrator. The librarians pointed out that such infrequent situations are not really problematic; because of the two-tier nature of the selection process, they still are not required to buy any particular title for their branches.

More distressing are the somewhat more frequent cases in which titles favorably reviewed by themselves and the Book Selection Committee are vetoed by the book selection head or the chief coordinator for reasons of unacceptable quality. Seven of the 14 interviewed branch librarians were particularly vocal regarding this tension between the two groups of librarians when asked about books that they want but cannot get. In the following representative response, one echoed her colleagues in disagreeing with the coordinators' primary emphasis on quality and, most particularly, with the influence of the latest publishing trends upon their selection concerns:

> I'm not sure [if there are any types of books we're not getting but need].
> . . . I can't think of a specific category right now. But I think they're [i.e., the people at the coordinating office] too quick to reject some things. And a lot of things are rejected for no good reason—only because there may be something a little better around that month or just because nobody cares about it enough to say, "Well, we should buy that." I think they're concerned a little too much with quality over popularity. Not just quality, but name authors and publishers and illustrators and things like that. Out in the branches, we don't think about publishers but in [the coordinating office] they do and they know what kinds of publishers are doing what kinds of stuff.

Generally speaking, however, the Metrosystem book selection process was seen as flexible enough to ensure coordinator control over the minimum requirements for acceptance, requirements ordinarily agreeable to branch personnel as well, while also mitigating much of the tension between the two groups with respect to the primacy of literary quality and popularity. The tension regarding titles of very high quality that branch personnel feel will not be popular in their branches is alleviated by allowing them to decide the particular books to purchase for their branches. At the same time, the chance that a book clearly unacceptable to coordinators will be deemed acceptable by branch librarians reviewers, thus exposing this undercurrent of tension, is reduced somewhat through a superficial screening of books on the part of the head of book selection before they are put up for review. Defending this activity with a rhetorical question, the head of book selection asked why she should waste a reviewer's time with an unnecessary title from an inferior publisher.

The Book Selection Guidelines

As might be expected in view of the previous discussion, the branch librarians (and even, to a lesser extent, two of the coordinators) emphasized different guidelines when reviewing books for system-level selection and when selecting books for their branches. Moreover, as might be expected, the guidelines expressed regarding the first tier, and noted in analyses of the division's review cards, were closer to those articulated in R&A than the guidelines expressed for branch choosing. Although tensions between coordinators and branch librarians over selection boundaries (tensions defined, in part, by the client relationship) were observed, the guidelines at the two tiers—like the perceptions of requirements at those levels—were generally consistent.

System-Level Selection

A comparison between the guidelines noted in the focal publishing organization and those articulated in Metrosystem regarding the reviewing of books at the first tier reveals strong compatibilities between the two groups of selectors. Metrosystem's spectrum of selection was observed to be somewhat broader than R&A's: while the editors and readers noted that they have tended to concentrate on fiction, the librarians evidenced a good deal of interest in procuring nonfiction titles that could be used by children to complete school assignments or for recreational reading.

The two groups of selectors were in tune regarding fiction, however. As in R&A, the outlet selectors noted plot, writing style, characterization, and illustrations (in picture books) as the most important content characteristics. Moreover, both emphasized similar guidelines with regard to these characteristics. The nonformulaic, individual nature of each title was stressed: broad leeway was allowed with regard to plot, required to be successful on its own terms; a personal style was demanded of the author and/or illustrator; depth and believability were required in characterization. Interestingly, the book selection head and others admitted that these guidelines are less stringently observed for nonfiction; accuracy and subject need were seen as paramount in that area. While these guidelines for nonfiction were also recognized by the editors, they tended to stress the importance of judging such titles for their literary quality.

In books about minorities, the two groups of selectors indicated the same approach. They said such books are actively sought, but noted that candidates would, in all but exceptional cases, have to meet the same standards of quality used to judge all entrees. Both groups also shared the same desire to improve the portrayal of women in children's literature, though without engaging in an activist campaign on the issue; for example, none of the librarians could remember the rejection of a book from the coordinating office because it was judged sexist.

The selection decisions made by R&A personnel in consideration of the economics of publishing also correctly predicted the preferences of the Metrosystem librarians. The pragmatic guideline of building the seasonal lists around names that have track records within the library market was mirrored in the librarians' admissions that, while they try to treat each title individually and would reject a name author if the material were poor, they do have predispositions towards books by generally esteemed figures.[3] Similarly, the publishing selectors were correct, at least in the case of Metrosystem, regarding librarians' predilection for a broad range of illustrations—not just those in color—and their willingness to pay for a handsomely produced book despite somewhat higher costs. In fact, when asked about price, the chief coordinator almost quoted the R&A promotion director: "It [i.e., price] doesn't matter because we're a public library. If it's a good book, we'll buy it."

On the more general level of format, R&A and Metrosystem agreed about paperbacks. Interestingly, the guideline of the library in this area shifted in response to the juvenile paperback revolution at approximately the same time that R&A began to produce its software line. Before the late 1960s, paperbacks could be bought for Metrosystem branches only if they were originals; the rule was subsequently changed to include all books already purchased in hardback (books that have thus gone through the evaluation process).

The strength of the library market client relationship between R&A and Metrosystem was even more evident in the aspects of content they both found unacceptable. One R&A editor and one reader noted a general, though not categorical, dislike for anthropomorphic characterization, a position taken by 7 of the 18 Metrosystem librarians. All the publishing and library selectors indicated grave reservations regarding series books and easy readers produced from word lists. Both groups justified their attitudes by designating such works as hopelessly formulaic in characterization, plot, and/or style. Cartoonish illustrations were similarly found generally unacceptable to the editors and librarians; "flat, noncommittal" books with Walt Disney characters were a particular target of attack by librarians. The latter had mixed opinions about abstract illustrations in juveniles, a pictorial approach usually avoided by R&A selectors.

Compatibility between publishing and outlet selectors was also seen in their guidelines regarding a title's moral point of view. Like the reader and editors, the librarians rejected books obviously dogmatic or moralistic. They were quite willing to accept curse words as long as they fit the context. Differences in discussing particulars of a moral point of view were evident, however. The formal policy and systematic reviewing procedure of system-level selection encouraged the library selectors to articulate their guidelines in a much more specific manner than that of their publishing counterparts. Several interviewed subjects recalled that certain types of books are specifically prohibited by the selection policy handbook: How-to manuals on subjects such as judo and hypnotism that "can cause serious injury to the reader unless carefully supervised by an expert" are excluded, as are titles relating to specific religious teachings or practice, since "the library considers the child's spiritual development as primarily the responsibility of his home and church."

Nonwritten guidelines espoused by the librarians were also more specific than those seen in R&A. The editors and reader generally followed the publisher in articulating such vague statements as "of course, if it's evil, we won't publish it." In contrast, the librarians found it easier, because of their public interest stance and training in writing critiques, to review the positive and negative points sought regarding a moral point of view. The following remarks by a branch librarian are typical:

> Well, we try to point out the themes in our review, not just give a capsule summary. What is the book getting at, what are its points. I think we try to point out if the book is straight out dogmatic and moralistic. We're not trying to moralize, I hope, or give books for children that we think will be "good" for them; but, on the other hand, we do like to emphasize positive values, you know? Values like "belief in yourself." Children need that kind of self-confidence to grow and learn how to handle things. And I think certainly we would like books about kindness more than books about people kicking other people in the face. So I think it comes through, although I hope it isn't that we just pick something that is a good value and no story.

The above-quoted librarian also echoed other respondents in pointing out that themes involving drugs, heterosexual activity, homosexuality, abortion, racial discrimination, race relations, and gang warfare have, along with curse words, been found in books accepted by the library. She noted, however, that such topics have been confined generally to titles for middle and upper-level juvenile readers, grades 4 through 8, and that books dealing with such problems should contain thoughtful, positive moral uplift even if they do not contain happy endings. A few librarians mentioned that the portrayal of explicit sexual activity is unacceptable.

Exceptions to these guidelines are sometimes allowed. The chief coordinator recalled that Metrosystem accepted a book for older children called *The Chocolate War,* containing a very depressing ending, because of the book's critical acclaim and its literary quality. She emphasized, however, that she instructed librarians who bought the book for their branches to read it and to recommend it only to emotionally mature readers. Parenthetically, the influence of the client relationship in broadening the library's acceptance boundaries regarding a moral point of view, an influence implicit in this example, is quite explicit in the following remarks made by the book selection head about the advent of so-called problem books:

> There are problem books—about what do you do when your parents are divorced, or conflicts of sexual feeling—that have come into books [within the past ten years], but it hasn't seemed to have affected us, because we've seemed to grow with it. I mean, it's fine, it's here, people are writing it, it's a good book, we'll buy it.

Branch-Level Selection

The librarians' emphasis on selection characteristics at the branch level showed a shift from a primary focus on the artistic aspects of content to a perspective that minimized the importance of critical acclaim and centered on the projected popularity of a title's subject matter or, more rarely, its author. The potentially negative consequence of this shift for the client relationship, however, was softened by the branch librarians' general commitment to literary quality, as well as by the fact that the system-level selection procedure determines the titles librarians can choose at the branch level. In fact, no guidelines articulated by the interviewed librarians regarding branch selection were incompatible with those seen in R&A; on the contrary, some similarities in criteria not found at the first level were observed. For example, the librarians' preferences regarding typography, binding, covers, and book size were identical to those of publishing selectors. In addition, the R&A promotion director's comment about librarians acting as buffers between publishers and communities were illustrated in branch personnel remarks about not avoiding the purchase of books passed by the coordinating office that have curse words or deal with controversial problems. Although the Metrosystem subjects agreed that complaints from parents are infrequent, they all outlined a specific procedure developed to cope with such incidents at the branch level. Three respondents, including the chief coordinator, mentioned that a primary reason for the division's written guidelines is to defuse extraorganizational criticisms by allowing the librarian to point to official policy as justification for a title's acceptance.

Conceptualizing the Audience

Intertwined with the librarians' discussions of their branch selection guidelines—and helping to shape those guidelines—was their image of the ultimate audience, the children. Actually, two perspectives on that audience, encouraged by the two fundamental requirements of popularity and quality, were apparent, with the coordinators emphasizing one view and the branch personnel stressing the other. Predictably, the coordinators' image was the most consonant with the approach of the major client relationship.

The Branch Librarians' Approach. The branch librarians saw children in terms of audience categories to be met during selection. As the R&A selectors predicted, the librarians used grade categories (preschool to 8) in their formal reviews; in their interviews and informal discussions, however, they tended to speak of both grade and age (3 to 12). Sex, reading ability and, in some cases, racial and ethnic backgrounds of the children were important to the librarians. While these categories were also mentioned by the publishing selectors, they were stated in more general and vague terms. The R&A editors did not appear to require specifics about their ultimate audience.

The librarians used their range of specified categories for selecting books to achieve a balance—the choosing of titles from a new book list so as to cover a wide range of audience slots. Popularity was often defined with balance in mind; it was taken to mean the high circulation of a title among the particular audience category for which is was intended. The following is an answer from the librarian of a moderately funded branch to a question about the guidelines she follows when choosing from the coordinating office selection list. It is representative of responses by other librarians, and illustrates how audience categories, conceptions of balance, and notions of popularity combine with budgetary considerations to shape selection at branch level:

> Despite the fact that we've gotten more money, the books have gone up in price, so you're where you were in the beginning. So you have to be very selective with regard to the books you buy. Very selective. You don't want to neglect one area to the exclusion of the other. You want to get books for the younger children. You want books for the boys. And there is a difference between the ages of, let's say, 8 and 12. No matter what people say, there is a very great difference in the likes and dislikes of boys and girls. So we have to get books which will satisfy the boys—say the sports books and so forth; they do like those kinds. Girls also like a special kind of story, which we call a "girl's story." Like *Little Women* and so forth. And then we have to get books for the preschoolers. We do have a lot of preschool books. But as I said before, that takes a lot of money. We're required to buy two copies of every picture book and easy reader. Which does make the budget a little difficult to manage. . . .
>
> We also try to balance the fiction and nonfiction titles. Not to have too many fiction to the exclusion of the nonfiction. I think most librarians try to get a balance. Of course that depends on the books that are up for order, to see if the balance is there. Of course, we do buy as we need. If we need

books on social studies and history—for example, this is a Bicentennial year—we buy more to cover that area because we get questions from children and teachers who come in.

All the librarians interviewed tended to prefer the same types of books for branch purchase—picture books and easy readers for the preschool and early grade children; monster books, joke books, sports books, automobile books, motor bike books, and books about World War II for older boys; modern romances and some fantasies for the older girls. Books with foreign dialects, taking place in foreign countries, or dealing with ethnic and racial groups not found in the branch area were avoided. Several respondents, noting the low reading level of the children in their branch areas, said that they tend to skew their purchases towards picture books and easy readers despite the need for balance. Generally speaking, the lower a librarian's budget and the poorer the reading ability of the area's children, the more she characterized as difficult any rigid adherence to the balance guideline and to the requirement of purchasing unusual books that are risky from the standpoint of popularity. One librarian was extremely concerned with circulation statistics, and noted in frustration that sometimes only the awareness of coordinating office scrutiny keeps her from buying "all joke books," since those titles tend to move the fastest and are most in demand.

The great majority of Metrosystem librarians did not aspire to take their concern for popularity to these ends, however. When the surveyed librarians were asked how often they "feel a conflict between the goal of maintaining a high quality and balanced collection and the goal of providing children with popular books which will constantly circulate," 14 (40%) said often and the rest (including the 3 responding coordinators) said sometimes. But, when asked to choose between four ways that they would prefer to resolve that tension, ranging from "a resolution fully on the side of popularity" or "quality" to "a compromise between the two goals but leaning towards the side of quality" or "popularity," all the respondents chose the compromise, with 40 percent, including the coordinators, leaning towards quality and 60 percent leaning towards popularity.

When articulating their concern for quality, the branch librarians subdued their demographic image of the audience somewhat and stressed a conception of children as having a particular generalized need—the need to be enriched with different types of special aesthetic experiences. The influence of the coordinators' and the client relationship's primary emphasis on aesthetics was clear here; many of the branch librarians said that they might purchase a title that the coordinators or the coordinating office reviewers judged as being of particularly high literary quality even if it did not promise to be immediately popular. Most added, however, that their decision would hinge upon two considerations—the number of other titles to be purchased in that month, and their estimation of whether they could sell the book to a fair number of their library regulars through individual recommendations made to children and/or parents, or through book talks. Some librarians made the influence of the client relationship upon their branch selection activities even clearer by noting that most branches routinely purchase the annual Newbery and Caldecott award winners, even though those titles have a reputation of not being terribly popular with children.

The Coordinators' Approach. While the branch librarians tended to accord the need for children's aesthetic enrichment as only a secondary consideration, the coordinators, more influenced by the client relationship, were quite explicit that this perspective was the most important one in their opinion. Since they had worked in the branches at one time and were continuing to order books for those outlets without children's librarians, they did see a practical necessity for audience categories. However, the specificity with which librarians discussed their branch children in terms of these categories was lost upon the coordinators, who admitted that they did not get out on the floor very much any more and must rely on feedback from branch personnel for information about what is popular.

Interestingly, the head of the System Coordinating Office played down the importance of specific information about the subjects and authors most popular for certain types of children in the branches. She interpreted the branch personnel's penchant for clearly popular titles as simply indicating that they prefer to choose "what seems to be what children want by what they say they want to take out," in view of the choices they have at the time. She went on to emphasize that the coordinators encourage the librarians to tap some of the less obvious possibilities for child literary enjoyment. High quality titles, she said, can be successfully introduced to children, especially if a good librarian is doing the introducing. This primary perspective on the ultimate audience would seem to favor the acceptance of titles from editors such as those in R&A, who view their child readers as sophisticated. Similarly, this perspective seemingly reinforces the coordinators' ties to the library market client relationship in general by making them more receptive to new literary-aesthetic experiences, defined as quality through the market's promotional apparatus.

The Conflict. The guidelines that librarians use for the coordinating office and branch selection procedures are usually compatible. During research for this study, however, certain incidents arose that illustrate how the contrasting primary emphases of coordinators and branch librarians upon quality and popularity, respectively, can lead to conflict between the two groups over the boundaries of acceptability. The sources of the controversy were the "Nancy Drew" series, picture books by Richard Scarry (who industry people say is currently the most popular children's book illustrator in the mass market), and easy readers with fixed word lists. Significantly, the books had been consistently rejected by the System Coordinating Office, while being constantly requested from branch librarians by many children and parents who had become familiar with them through nonlibrary sources.

The chief coordinator and the head of book selection treated each of the three problems in a somewhat different manner. Since knowledge about the requests for word list easy readers had not yet pervaded the system, the book selection head felt that explanatory action was premature. However, she seemed confident that such books, which she felt have a consistently stilted style, will continue to be rejected. In the case of Richard Scarry's books, which the coordinators considered repetitious and cluttered, demand on the part of branch librarians was very strong. Consequently, after two years of routine rejection, the coordinators agreed to accept one of his titles as a trial, ostensibly to gauge children's reactions to the much-vaunted books. Such a trial serves to circumscribe the acceptance of the title with an implicit notice that it is an exception, not a redefinition of the boundaries of quality. The labeling of the action as a trial also serves notice that it should not be taken as a precedent with regard to the evaluation of other Scarry books.

The coordinators refused to allow such a test with regard to the "Nancy Drew" fiction series, since the individual titles are numbered and to accept one would be to invite children to ask for the others. During an interview, the head of the coordinating office related that an angry letter from a large number of librarians petitioning her to allow the purchase of "Nancy Drew" books had precipitated her action to defuse the conflict. Convinced that the petitioners had not read a book from the series since their childhood, and evidently aiming to show the librarians that the newer editions are even worse than the older ones, the chief coordinator told all of them to read at least one old and one new "Drew" book (preferably the same title) before they met as a group to air their grievances. During the part of a bimonthly meeting that had been set aside for the "Drew" discussion, the head of book selection (who was substituting for the chief coordinator because of her illness) asked each librarian to state her opinion about the books she had read.

The tone of the collective comments approached that of a muted religious revival. One by one, the branch librarians stood, confessed that they had forgotten how poor the "Drew" books are, how much worse the new ones are than the old ones, and how the books do not belong in the library. It is, of course, impossible to know whether the format of the gathering influenced the comments of the librarians. Be that as it may, none of them spoke in favor of "Nancy Drew," either at the meeting or in the later survey questionnaire. The head of book selection, who had admitted her nervousness before the meeting, was genuinely relieved and thought it had gone well. The head of the coordinating office later predicted that the conflict would arise again in a few years. However, it seemed quite clear to her that she had successfully disposed of the popular mass market fiction series as a major subject of argument with her current group of branch librarians.

In answer to questions that specifically dealt with the differences of opinion between the coordinating office and the branches, one coordinator indicated that every organization has some tensions, and that these particular ones are cyclical occurrences precipitated when some young branch librarians are at their jobs long enough to "think they know it all." Speaking about the "Nancy Drew" series, the chief coordinator gave a pragmatic monetary reason for wanting to reject those books: if the system accepted them, the branches would continually be buying the series' many titles and replacing them as they wore out. The substantial money invested in this activity, she pointed out, would preclude branches from buying high quality books that deserve to be bought. It can be seen, then, that the quality guidelines championed by the System Coordinating Office—and reinforced by the client relationship—were triumphant in this revealing critical incident.

THE CLIENT RELATIONSHIP AND BOOK LISTS

The influence of the client relationship extended beyond the librarians' guidelines to the actual books they selected during the May 1974–April 1975 period.[4] Perhaps the clearest example of the preference that Metrosystem reviewers gave to library market products can be seen in a comparison of acceptance figures: while 48 percent of the 1,927 titles from library market firms was accepted for general branch circulation and 37 percent rejected, with the rest allowed just in the central or regional libraries, only 29 percent of the 96 mass market titles was fully welcome and 59 percent was rejected. This difference becomes even more significant in view of the head of book selection's remarks that the mass market firms send to the coordinating office only those books they feel are potential crossover material. Moreover, the acceptance of the mass market titles was predominantly (80%) in the realm of nonfiction. The librarians admitted that the area is judged less stringently than fiction from a literary quality standpoint. Indeed, nonfiction was seen to have a higher acceptance rate among books coming into the division: 45 percent of the 1,053 fiction and 51 percent for the 970 nonfiction titles.

64

Interestingly, Metrosystem's acceptance of the 53 R&A titles it received during the period studied was very close in percentage to its general acceptance of fiction, R&A's avowed forte and area of concentration. A breakdown of the System Coordinating Office rejections reveals that while 42 percent of the 50 fiction titles was accepted and 28 percent fully rejected, 2 of the firm's 3 nonfiction books were turned down. These results would seem to indicate that R&A has been correct to concentrate on fiction.

While the variety of R&A's fiction list matched the variety of fiction accepted by Metrosystem in terms of broad topics like fairy and folktales, adventure stories, sports stories, joke books, mysteries, and the like, the publishing firm's nonfiction list did not approach Metrosystem in diversity. This finding came to light in a comparison of coordinating office review files on all 316 titles accepted by the office in May, October, December, and March of 1974–75 with synopses of R&A titles released during that year.[5] In both lists, anthropomorphic characterization was rare, most books cost approximately five dollars, and fantasy titles were a minority among the fiction titles—though a 40 percent minority in Metrosystem and a 14 percent minority in R&A. Another noteworthy difference was the greater percentage of books for children 6 years or younger on R&A's list compared to Metrosystem's list (34% to 14%). This difference can be explained by two R&A editors' avowed preference for titles in picture book format, as well as by the librarians' reception of many nonfiction books designed to help older students with their schoolwork.

THE CLIENT RELATIONSHIP AND BRANCH SELECTION

R&A's books—particularly the firm's easy readers—were well-received at the branch level. While only 55 (31%) of all the sampled titles were purchased by more than 30 (57%) of the branches at one time, 11 (53%) of the accepted R&A titles had this distinction.

A closer look at the diverse purchasing patterns reveals that librarians did conform to their guidelines regarding branch selection. The desire for popularity is seen in the fact that picture books and easy readers were purchased by more branches than other books. By the same token, the number of branches purchasing fiction titles with foreign locales (which, librarians agreed, children avoid) was quite a bit smaller than the norm. Further analysis indicates, however, that at least one title with a foreign locale was chosen by almost every branch, presumably because of the librarians' attempts to conform to the guideline of balance. The same need for balance can explain the purchase of 1 or 2 of the 17 books with black characters by branches in predominantly white areas. It is noteworthy that almost all of the 17 titles were bought for the outlets in predominantly black neighborhoods.

Interestingly, in these cases of balance-motivated purchasing, librarians tended to lean more toward high quality books than to those that would obviously be popular. To a greater degree than the general sample, the titles with foreign locale or black main characters that had review cards marked excellent tended to be bought by more branches than titles with good or fair reviews. It appears that the guideline of balance became a vehicle for introducing books judged as having very high quality but doubtful immediate popularity. Here, too, the influence of the System Coordinating Office and, by extension, of the client relationship, can be clearly seen.

The continual interaction with publishers that has developed over the years does not dictate the primary organizational requirements that shape Metrosystem's selection of books. However, the client relationship does direct the coordinators, and through them the branch librarians, despite tensions between these two groups, towards fulfillment of those requirements in ways that reinforce the perspectives—and thus the power—of the market's dominant firms. Interestingly, the dominant library market perspective also has important consequences for the manner in which the librarians conceive of their ultimate audience. This situation, also seen in R&A, points to the notion that selectors' images of their audience are, to a large degree, molded by their perceptions of organizational demands and opportunities. While judging what is popular and unpopular is important, such judgments are determined within the confines of a spectrum of choice constructed because of the particular audience images the selectors hold.

This situation can be generalized. Just as its library market has a significant influence upon major publishing organizations, so the publishers influence the operation of major outlets to which they sell books. The influence of the relationship is two-directional: the producer-outlet interaction leads a production firm to gear its production around demands and opportunities defined by its major outlets, while at the same time it reinforces the dominant perspectives of the library market. Library selectors are guided in trends and issues by producers.

The library market client relationship has been seen to mold certain compatible guidelines, activities, and audience images with respect to children's books in both production and outlet organizations. The following chapters will examine how a very different client relationship shapes very different guidelines, activities, and audience images regarding what selectors in that segment also call children's books.

Part 2

The Mass Market

Chapter 4:   A Historical Preface

Nontext books for children have been sold to nonlibrary outlets since the early days of the American colonies. It was not until the middle of the nineteenth century, however, that such books began to be produced in large numbers and sold to different kinds of outlets, the so-called mass market. As the Preface to part 1 noted, one important impetus for this large-scale production of juveniles was the folding of the American Sunday School Union and the consequent decision by Sunday school librarians to purchase books on the open market. This development precipitated a flood of extremely inexpensive picture books for sale to the public through book-stores and dry good emporia, books usually unpromoted because their low profit margins did not make that feasible. The turmoil created by these cheap books among publishing firms was finally resolved for many of them in the relatively stable library market for juvenile books. The mass market continued to grow, however.

FROM DIME NOVELS TO MODERN SERIES

At the same time that the above-mentioned picture books for the very young were deluging stores, dime novels for adolescents were also extremely popular. These paperbacks were part of a general dime novel industry that had begun with the supply of inexpensive books to Union Army soldiers during the Civil War. Aside from selling the titles through magazine and newspaper outlets, the publishers took advantage of low postal rates to market them by mail as "libraries."[1]

The production of adolescent series books reached its climax in the nineteenth century in the firm of Street and Smith which, in addition to publishing many of Horatio Alger's works, released such extremely popular libraries as the "Frank Merriwell" series, "Nick Carter," and "Buffalo Bill." Each series was created by one of the firm's regular writers or editors under a pseudonym and was often continued by a staff of ghostwriters.

69

Among the firm's most prolific personnel were Alger, William Gilbert Patten, and Edward Stratemeyer. The latter, after he left Street and Smith, created the enormously popular "Rover Boys" series—thirty adventure stories that, beginning around 1908, Grosset and Dunlap sold for about fifty cents each and had sales that ultimately reached a total of five million copies.[2] The "Rover Boys" series was the forerunner of others that Stratemeyer and his ghostwriters produced in a similar style and between respectable hard covers, including "Tom Swift," "The Hardy Boys," and "Nancy Drew." The production of mass market adventure series books, continued in the unit Stratemeyer set up at Grosset and by others, has continued to the present.

DEVELOPMENTS IN PRODUCTION OF PICTURE BOOKS

The production of picture books for the mass market and the library market was profoundly affected by the adoption of new techniques in photo-offset lithography during the early 1930s that made possible books in full color at lower cost than ever before. Publishers in the two segments reacted very differently to the new developments. The library market firms emphasized the artistic possibilities that had now become economically feasible at library market prices and that its clientele would appreciate, while the goal of mass market firms was to lower the prices of color picture books to such a degree that a multitude of commercial outlets would feel that, if bought, the books could be sold to their Depression-ridden customers. Viguers has portrayed this difference from a decidedly library market perspective:

> The most spectacular development, then, between 1930 and 1940, was the great number and variety of picture books, and the profusely illustrated story books. There was no precedent for the latter, the very original picture-story books published during the first decade of lower reproduction costs. In a very few years, in the field of books for younger children, the artist attained a place of equal importance with the writer. In many cases, this necessary partnership of artist and author stimulated an artist to experiment in writing his own stories.
>
> An avalanche of merchandise, in lieu of literature, was to come, but not until after 1940. . . . It was not until a few years later, after the new developments were taken for granted, that sometimes a printer "turned publisher," and the mass production of picture books followed—bright in color, cheaply put together, with pictures and stories made to specific order.[3]

Actually, contrary to the above quote, production of mass market picture books in color was seemingly quite vigorous during the 1930s. They typically sold for 15 or 20 cents, as contrasted with approximately two dollars for the library market books. Two of the more notable firms active in this area, firms with their own printing plants, were Rand McNally and Western Publishing.[4] Of the two, Western was the most agressive with respect to mass market picture books, and by the beginning of World War II had cornered about 90% of the market through its Whitman imprint.

The virtual control that Western had on the sale of juvenile picture books in the mass market precipitated an interesting series of events in the 1940s that illustrates the influence of the client relationship on the product innovation process. The firm's officers were concerned that they were reaching the natural limits of expansion for the fifteen and twenty-cent Whitman books and that retailers were beginning to feel forced to buy Whitman because the competition in the field was so weak. At the same time, some bookstores and other outlets were not carrying the Whitman line because its very low prices made their profit margin unacceptable, or because they were not returnable if unsold.

Consequently, in an attempt to expand its market and set up its own competition. Western Publishing entered into an agreement with Pocket Books, Inc., to initiate a new imprint—Golden Books. Western agreed to create and publish the line while Pocket Books agreed to market it. Because the intention was to expand the market rather than to compete directly with Whitman, the firms agreed that the new imprint should signify higher quality than the older one, and that all Golden Books would retail at twenty-five cents. And, in order to further induce stores to carry the Golden line, the books were sold with a returnable provision.[5]

THE MASS MARKET TODAY

The expansion of Golden Books into many kinds of outlets, some of which had not carried the Whitman line, and the books' consequent success at the consumer level, changed the complexion of the mass market segment. By 1965, when Western took over the sales apparatus of Golden Books from Pocket Books, several firms had directly emulated or modified what had become the major juvenile book company's basic marketing procedure—orienting a wide range of titles and prices to a panoply of commercial distribution outlets, from bookstores to supermarkets. Interestingly, however, the particular nature of the client relationship that Western, along with Rand McNally and a few others, had cultivated during the 1930s and 1940s—a relationship based on the capabilities of large publisher-printers, on the general lack of advertising to the public about juveniles, and on the particular interests of the retailers with regard to quick, efficient, productive purchasing—had severely limited the ability of publishing firms to enter the field. As a result, only about six firms can be said to have significance in the mass market juvenile area. Moreover, the expansion of the market precipitated by the success of Golden Books has actually created several sectors within the mass market based on types of outlets, distribution routes used, and prices charged for the books. Some firms have chosen—or have been forced by economic circumstance—to concentrate on only a few of these areas.

The following two chapters will examine the consequences of the mass market client relationship for one important mass market publishing firm and two important mass market outlets—a bookstore chain and a department store chain. As in the case of the library market publishers, the influence of the major client relationship reaches to the core of the publishing operation by structuring, and thus delimiting, the range of necessary and desired activities for the firm when it chooses, produces, promotes, and markets its books. Similarly, though perhaps more subtly, the relationship has strong and important influences upon the bookstore and department store chains with regard to the books they choose, the manner in which they choose them, and the manner in which they sell them. While the same fundamental dynamic operates in both the mass market and the library market, a primary point will be underscored: the crucial differences between the two client relationships play an important role in instilling the selectors with quite different publishing perspectives and quite different definitions of a children's book—as well as with different images of the ultimate audiences that reflect those perspectives and definitions.

Chapter 5: The Mass Market
Publisher

Like R&A Publishing, Global Publishing operates under a "federal system": children's books are published by a separate division. In the more than thirty years that the company has produced children's books, the primary orientation has been towards the nonlibrary, predominantly bookstore market, although the percentage of its books that have crossed over to school and public libraries has been higher than most other mass market firms. During the past decade, however, a decision was made by the firm's executives to direct the juvenile division's activities much more clearly toward the mass market.

Two factors seem to have been most important in precipitating this conscious shift. Global's acquisition of two publishing firms with small but prestigious library market children's book divisions led to the realization that a more aggressive specialization by its children's division in the mass market, with books that could not cross over into the other segment, would allow the overall company to be in the enviable position of being successful in both segments. In addition, the budgetary problems of the library market in the early 1970s reinforced the growing opinion among Global executives that future expandability of the Children's Book Division lay in the direction of commercially, rather than publicly, sponsored outlets. At present, only about 10 to 15 percent of their new books end up in libraries, according to the publisher.

Global's Children's Book Division shares library and sales services with the firm's adult trade department. This arrangement was also used by R&A. However, the publishing companies have some very important differences in organizational structure that outweigh that similarity. The most striking difference, perhaps, is that while R&A's children's publisher is also an editor, her counterpart at Global doubles as the company's executive vice president in charge of marketing. Although Global's children's book publisher said that this dual position is a "historical accident," the sales manager and others mentioned the importance of the publisher's marketing expertise in helping the division respond quickly and properly to the mass market environment. In addition, interviews with editors and publishers from several mass market and library market juvenile divisions revealed that in virtually all cases the latter are headed by editorial people, while the former have market experts in positions of ultimate control.

Other important structural features differentiate R&A and Global. R&A's division has readers, while Global's does not, and Global's division has art directors while R&A's does not. Another fundamental difference relates to the compartmentalization of creative assignments: R&A personnel, ranked under the publisher as editors, associate editors, and readers, are not assigned to particular types of books, although some do have particular preferences. In contrast, Global's direct selectors under the publisher belong to four separate sections, called here "novelties/book clubs," "adolescent books," "paperback picturebooks," and "easy readers"; each section is responsible for the production of different "lines"—groups of titles in similar formats. The marketing control at the publisher level is matched in two of the sections by the presence of noneditor heads, who characterized their roles in terms of marketing rather than literary expertise.

These structural differences between the mass market and library market firms reflect appropriately different responses to very different perceptions of the major client relationship. The different responses, in turn, have fostered very different approaches to the definition and production of children's books. As a logical first step toward this goal, the Global selectors' understanding of the requirements and opportunities of their major client relationship must be examined.[1]

THE CLIENT RELATIONSHIP

The decision of Global's executives to position their Children's Book Division more clearly and aggressively in the mass market has already been noted. The importance of this orientation for the division's production of books was well understood by the eight direct selectors interviewed. They invoked particular aspects of their major marketplace to explain their book selection activities far more than their R&A counterparts. Taken together, their comments—and the comments by the other selectors—reveal an underlying conception of crucial requirements and opportunities mandated by the division's dealings with clients. Further analysis shows the broad considerations shaping this conception to be the same as those guiding the R&A selectors' understanding of their client relationship—the tradition of the publishing house and proclivities of the division's direct selectors; the environment of selection in, and the economic nature of, the marketplace; and the feedback and promotional environment. Because the particulars subsumed by these four considerations in Global's case are quite different from those seen at R&A, the conception of major requirements and opportunities posed by the client relationship is also quite different.

The history of the division and the strengths and weaknesses of the entire company have been of crucial importance in positioning Global in its current client relationship and directing its expansion. Of primary significance has been the trade book tradition of the entire firm. Western Publishing and Rand McNally both initially aimed their extremely low-priced juvenile lines at nonbook outlets and only later produced books at higher "price points" to sell to the bookstore trade. Global, in contrast, started out in the bookstore market, taking advantage of the firm's very effective sales force to introduce bookstore buyers and their jobbers to juvenile titles along with Global's extremely popular adult books. Instead of following other mass market firms in creating titles at a spectrum of price points attractive to various types of retailers and wholesalers, Global reflected its bookstore orientation by generally limiting the range of its prices and marketing its juvenile lines through names—either the names of author-illustrators who had spontaneously caught the fancy of consumers (some even crossed over into the library market), or names of popular characters from other mass media that would be instantly recognized by store customers.

This trade-oriented marketing approach has been very successful for Global children's books at the intended book, department, and large chain store level. Moreover, the division's particular success in the fantasy-adventure picture book and easy reader area, using its popular author-illustrators and characters from film and television cartoons, has involved it in the noninstitutional book club area of the mass market. Since the early 1960s Global has been party to a royalty arrangement to supply a large mail order book campany with six to eight titles each year for two book clubs. At the same time, however, the cost structure engendered by its trade-oriented approach has generally precluded the firm from expanding into the lower-priced sector of the market. In that sector independent distributors who, through their rack-service operations are the principal wholesale buyers for smaller outlets, demand a higher discount rate when purchasing than do the traditional trade book jobbers. It is a rate Global cannot afford.[2]

The past and present strengths and weaknesses of the Children's Book Division, then, have kept Global away from the sector primarily served by independent distributors and towards areas in which its large, 59 person, sales apparatus can function most effectively, such as book, department, large variety, and discount stores, plus any retailers served by jobbers, and toward the noninstitutional book club market. The hiring of two marketing-oriented vice presidents within the past five years, one of whom had worked for Western Publishing, to set up and head the "gimmick books" and "paperback picture book" sections of the Global Children's Book Division reflects the intentions of the publisher/marketing chief and the rest of the Global executive committee to expand their mass market operation.

A vestige of the division's tradition of purposefully crossing over into the library market with some of its books remains, however, primarily due to the interests of staff members from the "adolescent books" section. One member noted that the publisher, recognizing that they would like to produce an occasional library market book ("a book book," she called it), allows them one or two such titles a year for morale purposes.

The Marketplace

In reviewing Global's publishing tradition, some economic aspects of the marketplace that helped selectors form their conceptions of the requirements and opportunities posed by the major client relationship were discussed. These considerations direct the firm's planners toward areas within the mass market where the division can have maximum control over its chances for success. The present section will outline some of the particular considerations within that chosen marketplace seen by the interviewed participants as raising certain requirements and opportunities with regard to the client relationship.

One important similarity between the mass market selection environment and the library market selection environment is the general lack of sustained advertising and promotion by publishers to their potential reader audience. Global's sales manager illustrated the public's unfamiliarity with children's books by pointing out three kinds of titles that are competitive at their points of purchase—dictionaries, Bibles, and children's books. Generally, he said, consumers come upon such books with few, if any, preconceived notions of the particular editions they want. The R&A selectors deal with this situation by placing their trust in librarians to review, search out, and highlight good books and introduce appropriate titles to children and their parents. Global's selectors, in sharp contrast, emphasized that no agent of the publishing firm is present in the book or department stores to introduce books to customers.[3] In fact, they stressed that clerks in most stores carrying Global titles have little knowledge about children's books and are either not prepared or lack the time to introduce particular titles on particular subjects to curious browsers.

Because of the presumed point of purchase nature of children's book selection and the lack of knowledgeable agents to suggest choices to children or their parents, the display pattern of the titles is important. To catch the potential customer's eye, most distribution oulets display their picture books on racks or flat out on tables. The racks are walled or free-standing, with free-standing ones sometimes supplied as promotional devices by the publisher. Due to lack of space, and based on the idea that readers will search them out, nonpicture books for adolescents have generally been shelved spine out, although some outlets place them with covers showing so as to make them more visible to impulse shoppers. A few selectors pointed out that while adolescent titles—particularly those in series—sell quite well, preschool materials are the most important items in the mass market. The head of the "gimmick books" section opined that "young adults who read, read adult books."

Global's marketing, sales, and editorial personnel noted that the absence of effective, personal in-store aid for potential book customers has brought about a demand on the part of buyers (distribution outlet or jobber agents who buy books from Global) that books essentially sell themselves. Lines and individual titles that have proven their abilities in this regard are bought repeatedly by outlets; a good backlist is therefore a valuable commodity for a mass market publisher.

Global's selectors agreed, however, that new books are welcomed by buyers, on the chance that the new titles might sell themselves more successfully than the older ones. They noted that the buyers judge the potentials of new books by gauging their similarities to those currently successful within the mass market environment in terms of format, cover attractiveness, subject, illustrative style and, in a very limited number of cases, the author-illustrator. The importance of a book's similarity to others with good mass market track records was underscored in their pointing out that it is much easier to sell a new title to a store or jobber representative if it is introduced as an addition to a popular line. One salesman said that the concept of a line is at least as important as a device for getting books into stores as it is for achieving recognition and sales at the ultimate consumer level. And, in the words of the paperback picturebook section head, "if you can get them in [stores, particularly enough stores to justify the necessarily low price of the book] you can sell them."

The Importance of Price

The economic considerations of Global clients were also noted by marketing and sales personnel as creating demands and opportunities with respect to their client relationship. Retailers have found, they said, that customers are extremely sensitive to the prices of children's books. The publisher opined that people probably do not even look at the number of pages they get for their price; they simply look at the price. Moreover, he said, comparative sales figures have shown that customers prefer picture books with full-color illustrations over those which are not in full color.

Global's sales manager agreed with a suggestion that these presumed customer preferences might well be a consequence of the presumed point of purchase ignorance on the part of parents and children as to what constitutes a good children's book. Perhaps because they have few, if any, preconceptions regarding definitions of quality in juveniles, color and price become major considerations. The "novelties/book club" section vice president suggested that low price is especially important to parents with very young children, since they tear and eat their books. Of more concrete and immediate significance to the selectors, however, was the fact that store buyers judge full color and competitively low price points (from under $2 to a maximum of about $4.95 except in unusual cases) as crucial factors for salability.

The publisher and two salespeople noted that, even within their chosen sector of the mass market, different retailers require different price points with respect to juveniles. Lower ticket items, usually $2.50 or less, are preferred by variety chains and less expensive department stores because the buyers feel their customers will not pay more. On the other hand, bookstores and department stores with book sections tend to shy away from Global's lower priced products because the titles will not, they feel, bring in a high enough per unit profit, even with brisk sales, to justify the use of space that could carry higher profit items that moved at a similar—or even slower—pace. For example, one salesperson pointed out that the division's 95¢ paperback picturebooks, designed as low ticket items for the variety stores, are not bought by some bookstores despite their good sales records in various outlets. He noted that New York's Brentano's puts the Global paperbacks in the basement, away from the main juvenile section. Scribner's, another prestigious New York bookstore, refuses to stock those titles during the pre-Christmas season, an especially high turnover time when space is very precious, but does carry them at other times of the year.

The Influence of Response and Promotion

Global selectors' understanding of the environment in which they receive responses about old books and promote new ones amplified and extended their conceptions of the limits of their marketing and creative opportunities regarding the division's client relationship. Advertising in trade journals such as *Publishers Weekly* was judged a routine necessity to prepare buyers for new titles and to reinforce the firm's name. However, the promotional and information-gathering activities of most consequence were thought to be those carried out by the company's 54 salespeople—the division's most direct link to its outlet buyers. Assigned to particular territories throughout the country, these publishers' representatives call upon their store and jobber clients at least twice a year to sell them the new Global adult and children's titles for the fall and spring seasons. Their formal feedback is present in the periodic reports they send to the sales manager.

Several selectors noted that buyers, who often have only minor interest in children's books, do not want to be bothered with considerations of single titles and prefer to deal with a firm that has a well-developed assortment of children's lines, or books grouped around similar formats. The high cost and difficulty of initiating such a program usually ensures that Global will continue to have only about three or four major competitors in its market sector. Marketing and sales personnel proudly observed that salespeople visiting jobbers or store buyers have the full weight of the company's name behind them, a promotional asset enhanced by the impressive track records of the division's variously priced lines. In fact, they said, salespeople who service major accounts such as jobbers and large department stores do not usually talk to buyers in terms of individual titles; rather, they deal in terms of "programs"—packages of Global children's books that the salesperson has tailored to the turnover and profit requirements of the store and keyed to the previous year's success in terms of sales and returns.

An interviewed salesperson who services minor accounts indicated that she, too, fills out Global children's book order lists for buyers who know and have learned to trust her, although in the case of forthcoming titles she might be asked to exhibit the cover and other samples supplied by the production department. Gaining buyer confidence, she noted, is a consequence of successfully servicing an account—knowing the requirements of the store in terms of "turns" (the amount of time required to sell out the stock profitably), knowing what mix of books will move quickest, knowing how to reorder and what books to pull because they are not turning.

The Global Children's Book Division publisher noted that it is very difficult for him to rely on the feedback of salespeople about the marketability of proposed new lines and formats, because the vagaries of individual salesperson temperament make it difficult to determine how realistic their predictions are as to buyer reactions in their territories. Consequently, when important, large-scale decisions are made, the publisher contacts the buyers from some of the firm's major accounts to determine their receptivity to the new ideas. Those buyers are routinely cultivated by inviting them to the annual company-wide sales meeting, often held at a resort location, in which all the firm's new fall titles are introduced to the sales staff. In the case of an expensive new project, an enthusiastic buyer might even be asked to guarantee purchase of the proposed titles.

In general, however, salespeople are the most important vehicles for getting Global children's books into the stores and to the jobbers. This situation places the marketing executives (the publisher and his section vice presidents) in the interesting position of having to convince their sales force of the self-salability of the division's new titles. And, generally speaking, the close contact between salespeople and buyers—and the commitment of the former to maximize the latter's sales—seems to lead to caution on the part of these publishers' representatives with regard to new books. A few of the direct selectors, as well as one salesperson, noted that new titles and lines are welcomed only if they are solidly anchored to popular subjects, illustrative styles, and author-illustrators. The salesperson conceded that he and his colleagues might sometimes be more conservative in this regard than the buyers themselves. This situation would seem to be a further incentive for Global's marketing and creative people not to stray too far from the elements of previous success.

A comparison of the way Global and R&A selectors conceptualized the requirements and opportunities of their respective client relationships reveals striking differences. The library market respondents saw themselves as working within a vaguely definable good book tradition that emphasized individuality and literary quality and would accept unusual productions from editors with the proper reputation and promotional apparatus. In contrast, the mass market respondents drew a picture of a marketplace more explicit in its demands, much less open to unusualness or idiosyncrasy. While both groups of selectors articulated the importance of a track record, the R&A personnel saw it as helping to ensure a book's favorable reception, while the people from Global saw the notion as virtually the sine qua non of selection. And, whereas the emphasis in the library market was on single titles encouraged by thriving review media, the emphasis in the mass market was on lines, programs, and lump monetary sums.

These strong and seemingly fundamental differences begin to explain the structural differences found between the two firms. The literary perspective and promotional techniques encouraged by the library market would seem to guide the choice of a juvenile publisher in that market to someone conversant with the literary tradition of that market and whose reputation will help promote the division's titles. At the same time, the merchandising point of view and promotional techniques of the mass market would seem to demand a marketer as publisher—someone conversant with the tactical considerations that lead jobbers to accept new books and lines, and store buyers to put them on their shelves. Also when lines, rather than individual titles, are the preoccupation of a juvenile division, the most efficient approach would be to assign individuals to specialize in producing books that conform to particular types—a situation found in Global Publishing.

SELECTING AND PRODUCING BOOKS
FOR THE MASS MARKET

The Global selectors' concepts of requirements and opportunities in their client relationship set the stage for a publishing process that attempts to create books that will be welcomed by salesmen, store buyers, and jobbers alike. In addition, the structure of the division, in terms of occupational designations and relationships, can be seen as a response to these notions. This suggestion is supported by the discovery that differences between the structures of Global and R&A seem to parallel, and thus be rooted in, fundamentally different perceptions of the demands and freedoms of the marketplace by the firms' selectors.

The following discussion supports these propositions by showing how the Global selectors' understanding of their client relationship requirements and opportunities have consequences for the firm's entire publishing process—from the responsibilities of principals involved to their guidelines regarding the formulation of seasonal lists, lines, and titles.

The Client Relationship and Selection

A significant indication of the fundamental differences in approach between R&A and Global—and the different influences of the client relationships—is that the degree of these divisions' dependence on their firm's marketing and sales departments was characterized in polar opposite terms. The R&A marketing director noted that its children's division is almost independent of these forces, while Global's trade sales manager said that its children's division is almost dependent upon them. This difference is quite understandable; the main spur to sales in the library market lies not in the initiative of the sales force but, rather, in the initiative of the editorial and promotional staff, who create an environment of acceptance, and of the librarians themselves, who read the books—or the reviews—and then send specific orders to jobbers.

An understanding of the firms' different approaches to their client relationships also helps explain why the two groups of selectors expressed different attitudes towards the size of their seasonal lists, despite the fact that in both divisions list size was seen as a function of the general economic conditions in the trade and size of the divisional budget. Because their books are often sold in programs based on previous sales and without reference to specific new titles, Global selectors indicated quite a bit of concern with tying the sizes of their lists to particular reports of the money that buyers are willing to lay out for juveniles. They also noted that a greater number of books are produced for their fall list, because store buyers tend

81

to order more juveniles for the pre-Christmas season. In contrast, R&A's list size is approximately the same for each season, since library budgets are not dispersed in any systematic, semiyearly pattern. Library market selectors, convinced as they were that their traditional quota of good books will sell under a wide latitude of economic circumstances, noted that fluctuations in library revenues have not shortened their seasonal lists.

General Selection Procedure

When looked at from a broader perspective, the different client relationships bring about important differences in the firms' book selection activities. R&A's procedure—previously described as a response to perceived demands and freedoms posed by its client relationship—is literally a selection process, in which readers and editors choose manuscripts written by house authors, known talent, or even over-the-transom discoveries, with the publisher/editor acting both as confirmer, making sure that a manuscript is a feasible good book, and overseer, making sure that a list is balanced. At Global, however, the client relationship encourages a selection process whereby the overwhelming number of titles are not selected from those proffered to the division. Rather, the works are originated in-house at the specific request of the publisher/marketing director, by the editors, section heads, and the publisher himself. Moreover, in cases where the books are not initiated by Global's direct selectors, they usually originate from the firm's name author/illustrators, who are under long-term contract with the firm and whose names bespeak a track record to salespeople and buyers alike. The editor/art director in the novelty books section explained the in-house initiation of titles in terms of the marketplace:

> We almost always come up with ideas [for books] ourselves. Occasionally someone will come to us with an idea. It's not that we're closed to it. It's that we know what we want and what sells.

Global's book selection procedure generally takes place in the following manner: at a particular time during each season, the publisher will ask his section heads to present proposals for their sections' contributions to a list a few seasons away. Sometimes he might tell them how many books from each of their lines he needs; at other times he might wait for their suggestions and then decide. In either case, the section head will solicit ideas from his editors, art director, or both and, after screening out unfavorable suggestions, he will present his choices to the publisher.

After an idea for a title is tentatively accepted, the book must be justified as to its profitability at a projected competitive price. This justification procedure involves the sales and production departments, as at R&A. However, whereas the competitive prices in the library market (reaching $7 and $8 for slim, full-color picture books) allow R&A to project sales of 10,000 copies for a 3-color book (except easy readers) and 20,000 copies for one in full color, Global's virtual requirement for full color with prices below $5 mandate sales projections quite a bit higher, usually ranging from 35,000 to 100,000, the latter for the 95¢ paperback picturebooks.[4] The existence of book lines at Global makes the justification procedure somewhat easier than in the library market, because a new title retains the same format (and costs, accounting for inflation) of the others in the line and, it is hoped, a similar sales potential.

When the ideas are approved for publication, the section heads, editors, and art directors must carry out the projects. Their particular activities vary depending on the section and line involved. They can range from the editor's actually writing the book and then finding, or allowing the art director to find, an appropriate or customary artist, to a section head's informing one of the firm's name author/illustrators that a book in a particular format is needed, and directing the course of that work to publication. The purpose in all activities is to conform to the perceived mandates of the client relationship as efficiently as possible.

Selection Guidelines

Global's publisher observed, while talking about the firm's two library market subsidiaries, that "by decreeing their books will sell only 10,000 copies [and thus pricing them out of the mass market] we are committing a self-fulfilling prophecy. It's kind of strange, really." However, he later reversed this sentiment by opining—as did several other people who produce children's books—that library market books could not really sell themselves in the mass market and, in most cases, would not get past the buyers to be given a chance; thus, projected higher sales could not materialize. Other experienced observers and participants from both segments of the industry added that library market royalty rates and production standards, particularly with regard to format flexibility and binding, impose higher costs on library market books that would not make them competitive even if the same quantities could be sold.

Mass market publishers, then, utilize selection guidelines that take full advantage of their access to the mass market. In the process, differences other than price that separate the two segments become quite clear.

The Existence of Lines. The concept of a line of books, the core of the Global Children's Book Division selection and production process, has been related to considerations of client relationship. The crucial importance of lines for successfully introducing new juvenile books to buyers has already been noted. Lines are also deemed important for aiding the division's titles to sell themselves in the stores, since a customer familiar with previous books of a line might more readily purchase a new one from that line. In the economics of publishing for the mass market, lines have already been mentioned in connection with justification, which is made easier if a proposed book is fit into the same format and same potential sales track as previous titles. In addition, the production of books in similarly formatted groups is also meant to conform to the mandate of the client relationship for a competitively low price: the fact that a similar size, binding, paper quality, typography, and general layout are associated with each line means that much less design work is required, saving these expensive start-up costs. Note that these standardizations—and the cost rationale—were also seen in R&A's easy readers, aimed towards a healthy bookstore sale.

Unlike R&A Publishing, however, where any editor can work on an easy reader, Global has separate sections devoted to different lines of books. Each section actually produces more than one line; the lines are assigned to or originated by the sections because of their similarities in format to existing section specialties. Thus, the novelty books section's vice president and editor/art director originates a "pop-up book" line, a "mix and match" line, "cut-out" books, and, in the words of an art director, "all those books which are the middle ground between toys and books." The paperback picturebook section head, with the help of an art director, produces the division's "pictureback" and "board book" lines; the "adolescent books" section originates a nonfiction sports line assigned exclusively to the senior editor and a mystery-adventure series assigned exclusively to the managing editor[5]; and the "easy readers" section produces two lines of easy readers, one of which is a fantasy-adventure series.[6]

The fact that these nine lines encompass the great majority of children's books produced by Global each season and are pegged at prices ranging from 95¢ to about $4 reflects the observation by selectors that store and jobber agents tend to purchase from firms with an assortment of differently priced lines. The orientation of most of the lines towards the preschool age is also understandable in view of the interviewed subjects' claim that young children and their parents are the predominant audience in the mass market. The division does put out "unattached" titles, books that do not fit into these lines. The books usually have elements that will cause the buyers to feel they will sell themselves in their outlets.[7]

Two questions arise in this connection: What kinds of content do Global selectors perceive as making their lines and titles most likely to succeed in the mass market? and, What guidelines do the selectors follow regarding that material?

Global's selectors all saw the book's subject as quite important to the book's success. R&A selectors felt the same way. However, while the R&A respondents refused to indicate specific preferences for subjects and stressed that they lean toward the unusual and innovative, Global respondents found it quite easy to set forth their guidelines, which emphasize the most traditional juvenile subjects. Nonfiction sports books about heroes or famous moments and adventure-mystery stores about continuing characters are the primary adolescent material, directed at ages 10 and up, while unattached activity books are aimed at middle-aged juveniles, ages 8 and up. As for the subjects of the mass market's most important area, picture book fare for young children, the "gimmick books" editor/art director echoed her colleagues:

> Cats and dogs are always going to go. Children prefer animal books—cute cuddly animals; they prefer Mother Goose, fairy tales. [The paperback section head added that the fairy tales should be ones most commonly known.] The standard juvenile fare are the best sellers.

As the quotation implies, the editors and marketers felt that the subjects chosen for their division's books should be presold to the consumer: the parent or older child walking down the store aisle should not have to read the book or a long review of it to find out what it is about. Subjects that do not have this instant appeal—notably poetry (beyond short rhymes) and whimsical fantasy—are not produced. "They're harder to get through. They're harder to get through to the house here, through the salespeople, the [stores'] buyers—everybody," one art director explained.

Another fairly evident aspect of picture books that is thought to help the titles sell themselves to parents is the blending of educational information into the material, to make its value for the child quite explicit. Most often this blending is done at the book, rather than the line, level. For example, the novelty books editor, who writes that section's works herself, mentioned that in scripting a "pop-up" book about trains she had decided to combine "a little of fact and a little of fancy" on the subject. In the case of the division's easy readers, however, the instructional approach is built into the line: the authors are required to use a fixed word list prepared by Global's educational books division. In contrast, both the production and distribution outlet selectors from the library market noted their dislike for easy readers with predetermined vocabulary.

Simultaneous with their attempt to build lines around presold subjects that invite point of purchase interest, the selectors are also extremely careful not to inject any elements into their books that might possibly turn potential customers or potential store agents away. In striking contrast to R&A's products, curse words are unknown in Global's books. The "gimmick books" editor echoed her colleagues claim that "we try not to do anything [in questionable taste], even such words as 'ain't.'" She also stated that titles in the library market's problem book vogue "are unnecessary. A lot of it is sort of proving they [i.e., the library market authors and publishing firms] can deal with topics that have not been dealt with."

Style, Authors, and Plots. Such remarks imply that writing style, considered extremely important in the library market, was not deemed important at Global. Indeed, the mass market selectors seemed to feel that since style is not evident to the buyers who, unlike librarian reviewers, do not read the books nor probably to the customers, who are sold immediately by the subject or other visible track record elements, it could be used to help lower book costs. This feat is accomplished by having the editors themselves, rather than the firm's four name author-illustrators, write picture books. With the lengthier adolescent titles, cost-cutting is accomplished by providing formulas for writers, so that books can be turned out quickly for a set fee rather than a royalty, or for a very small royalty.

The adventure-mystery editor, in characterizing the formula for her line (which revolves around the activities of "three adventurous young sleuths"), noted that its creator died several years ago and the books are currently written by two ghostwriters. She said that she tries to make sure that stylistic differences are not detectable. The editor also observed that the protagonists' ages are never presented "so that the readers will more easily identify with them." Format requirements of the line mandate that the story be told in either 160 or 192 pages. Moreover, each book contains a list of the other books in the series. The hope is that a child who buys one title will go to a store and ask for another from the list, even if neither the line nor the book is prominently displayed.

The senior editor was also quite specific about the formulas used in his nonfiction, 160-page sports books, for which he commissions reliable professional sportswriters:

> It's been our practice since the beginning to put into a book several profiles of players, or several great moments—a group of maybe 6, 8, 10, or 12 in a book. It gives us the opportunity to achieve some geographical distribution. We've discovered over a period of time that that's a smart thing to do in a mass market book, because it gives it a certain amount of appeal everywhere. . . .
>
> The formula for a profile is usually this: It will begin with sort of a dramatic lead. A game situation in which our hero has won the game, or maybe a heartbreaking situation in which he has lost the game. Something that kind of provides the theme, the peg on which to build. And then, usually, there's a line space or some kind of a break, and then you go back to his early life. And you end up his last season. And, because of the unhappy

way that the sports and publishing seasons don't get along, we like to have the last season up near the end so that we can add to it at the last minute.

A list of other books is also found in each sports line title.

Illustrations and Illustrators. While distinctive writing style was considered only minimally important to Global's books, illustrations, highly visible selling points, were considered extremely important. In fact, the standout importance of pictorial presentation helps explain why Global has separate art directors. In contrast, the balanced importance of written material and illustrations in R&A's picture books is reflected in the fact that its editors also perform the traditional art director's role of evaluating potential talent and guiding a book's artwork to its completion.

Not only was the relative emphasis of the pictorial and the literary different in the two firms; the actual guidelines for illustrations were quite different as well. Although the mass market respondents contend that they, like the library market selectors, are looking for individual styles, the styles they preferred as mass market—cartoonish, bright, bold, and direct, with the cover "like a poster"—would, by their own admission, be generally unacceptable to many librarians. When asked to compare their guidelines to those of R&A's library market subsidiaries, both interviewed art directors added "slightly less sophisticated" and "perhaps more humorous" to the above list.

As a consequence of these guidelines, the art directors noted that they generally look for artists with different styles from those who work in the library market, although their preference for artists who are reliable with regard to scheduling and completing work are similar. Most desirable, of course, is the small number of author-illustrators whose names are synonymous with popularity to buyers, to the extent that the names become principal track record elements for titles. (One library market salesperson might have overestimated the number of name mass market author-illustrators at 12.) In view of the insignificant amount of nontrade related advertising allocated to the division, Global's marketers do not attempt to create a following by widespread promotion of particular favored talents. Instead, they rely on sales reports and salespeople's observations to determine the author-illustrators considered self-salable by buyers, and attempt to capitalize on those successes through the release of more titles by those talents, highlighting their names on the covers. Because of Global's tradition of cultivating such name author-illustrators, the division actively pursues important talent, offering royalties high by mass market standards. Illustrators not so well known are usually contracted per book and offered typical mass market royalties or fees.

Comments by Global's direct selectors seem to indicate that if a title's content characteristics, in terms of subject, color use, price, format, and character identifiability, are deemed to provide strong enough track record and low price factors to allow the book to sell itself easily, the added royalty expense of an important author-illustrator might not be necessary. An example is the "pop-up" and "mix and match" lines, where the technically well-produced novelty formats are felt to be the principal track record elements. On the other hand, one of the division's easy reader lines has always been tied to the firm's name talent, providing the line with an enviable track record throughout the division's sector of the mass market.

Characterization. Character identifiability has been called a track record element. To Global selectors, some of the most important characters in their books are those from other mass media—principally television, newspaper comics, and comic books. They and buyers consider these characters immediately recognizable to children and their parents. While the library system resisted these personalities as commercial and/or cartoony, characters from Walt Disney Productions, "Peanuts," "Mister Rogers' Neighborhood," "Sesame Street," and other nonbook origins are licensed in various forms of exclusivity throughout the mass market.

In Global, the line of fantasy-adventure easy readers, also sold through a mail order firm's book club, is built around famous cartoon characters, with an editor writing the stories and ghost illustrators imitating the licensing studio's artists. Presold characters are additionally used in unattached productions such as activity books and calendars. The objective is to get those relatively common subjects of the middle-aged juvenile area stand out from their competitors in the eyes of buyers and consumers. The sports line follows the character identifiability notion by emphasizing stars in the books, while the adventure-mystery line does so by using a famous name from adult mysteries in the line's title and through the series device of maintaining continuing characters in all the episodes. It should be noted, however, that while character identifiability was considered important among selectors, depth and subtlety of portrayal—crucial among library market selectors—was not mentioned as a guideline by the mass market subjects, and was specifically denied by the mystery-adventure series editor.

Another predilection of R&A's selectors—unusual, nonmainstream characterization—was also not found at Global. The latter group, like the former, did indicate a sensitivity about portraying women in a manner that balances traditional and nontraditional roles, and about including blacks among the characters in picture books. Moreover, the senior editor noted that although he tries to balance the race of athletes in his sports books, the predominance of blacks in basketball sometimes necessitates a predominance of them in a book and on the cover. However, focusing upon racial or ethnic group members in a nonsports framework—and particularly at the picture book level—was rare. The "adolescent book" section's art director spoke for her colleagues when she explained this situation by stating: "Because we're aiming at the mass market, we sometimes turn down a book everybody likes because we feel its appeal is too narrow."

Interestingly, the fear of injecting into books elements that might turn potential customers and buyers away was related by the novelty books editor to the predominant use of animals as main characters in picture books:

> It's easier. You don't have to determine if it's a girl or boy—right? That's such a problem today. And if it's a girl, God forbid you put her in a pink dress. Also, it's very hard to draw children in—how can I put it? Here, for example, in this book the children are cartoony. Now, if you were to draw more realistic children, the whole book would somehow get a little heavier, a little more serious. You have to keep your characters a little lighter, a little more whimsical. And animals lend themselves to that.

Format. A final area of content affected by the client relationship is the format of the book. The production of books in lines is deemed important by Global selectors for introducing books to buyers, achieving self-salability with customers, and lowering production costs. The "adolescent books" are director concisely explained how the client relationship's low cost mandate has influenced decisions regarding different facets of format:

> Over the years, if you want to print mass market, you try to cut every penny you can and print more than one book at a time for economy at the production end of it. And they [the publisher, appropriate section head, and production department] have evolved certain formats which are economical as far as the kind of press it's going to be on, the kind of paper, and the size of the paper.

Other production procedures intended to lower costs while not impairing the point of purchase marketability of the books include avoiding unusual and expensive typography; dispensing with cover jackets by using laminated or "kivar" covers to achieve the same promotional effect; and providing cemented ("perfect") or stapled bindings, rather than regular trade bindings.

The dimensions and number of pages of the books in a Global children's line are arrived at by attempting to optimize both production cost efficiency and the contribution of size as a track record element. The novelty books editor observed that store buyers and their customers become accustomed to seeing certain types of books in certain sizes. A frequent example is the firm's two lines of easy readers which are, at 6½ by 9 inches and 6⅝ by 9¼ inches respectively, small as compared to most picture books, because such titles are expected to fit easily into the hands of children. By contrast, the division's standard picture books, called "flats," are quite a bit larger than its easy readers, because they have been found to sell better if larger. A Global salesperson said that the large size of these flats is due to the trend-setting and competition-inciting activities of Western Publishing, which uses oversized presses especially designed to produce books that command attention.

Interestingly, the competition for attention on the store racks among large picture books was confronted directly by Global's marketers when they decided to create the paperback picturebook line. They were convinced that original picture books with name author-illustrators and track record subjects would be attractive at 95 cents to agents of lower-priced variety and chain stores. However, because of production costs, they were unable to produce a size larger than 6 by 6 inches. Consequently, they decided to follow the fairly common procedure of convincing buyers to accept the books with spinner racks. The free-standing, round racks are aimed at separating the line from the larger hardback juvenile crowd and giving it a much better chance to sell itself to store customers.

Thus Global's guidelines regarding format, like those regarding other important areas of content, are at variance with the guidelines reported for R&A Publishing. There, in a process shaped by selectors' perceptions of the requirements and opportunities of a different client relationship, titles were discussed as individuals—as the most artistic economically feasible package of subject, story, writing style, illustrative style, and format elements. Only the easy readers contained aspects of the line concept in their production procedure.

At R&A, the influence of the major client relationship extended beyond the articulation of guidelines by the selectors to their very images of their ultimate audience and the actual books they release in the seasonal lists. A similar dynamic was observed at Global Publishing, though with different results reflecting the different nature of the client relationship.

THE CLIENT RELATIONSHIP AND
THE ULTIMATE AUDIENCE

The general notion of preselling a book to parents or children found in remarks by Global personnel, and the particular comments they made regarding content children or parents like or do not like might, on the surface, be taken to imply that the selectors have concrete images of their ultimate audience based on direct audience data. Actually, however, when the direct selectors were asked about the images they have of the people who read their books, all uniformly denied any knowledge of their ultimate audience. The novelty books section head observed that no market research is done, for reasons of costs, and that "we're really flying by the seat of our pants." The senior editor characterized as "parlor wisdom" the Global selectors' assumption that a parent usually chooses the book for a younger child with or without the child present, and that adolescents have more access to books on their own.

Nevertheless, the selectors articulated guidelines and operated as if they had clear impressions of their ultimate audience. As at R&A, that impression reflected the selectors' perceptions of the requirements and opportunities of their client relationship. The requirement of store and jobber buyers for low price and high turnover is interpreted by Global selectors as a mandate to reach the widest possible audience. Moreover, the content elements used to reach this audience are usually chosen from the spectrum of previously successful materials—the buyers' concept of track record.

Because of the healthy sales of their division's books, Global personnel contended that the books they publish are generally the books children want. The firm's promotion director even stated that mass market books are more likely to give children what they want than those oriented to the library market:

> The book has to be designed for the child. What's happened in the library market is that frequently people are directing themselves in creating fine, fine literature which appeals to adults, who are the intermediaries in the libraries. Because the ultimate consumer is kind of unknown, hidden. In the bookstore the ultimate consumer is not hidden. If the kid didn't like the book, the mother is not going to come back.

An almost exactly opposite opinion was stated by a library market editor.

THE CLIENT RELATIONSHIP AND THE SEASONAL LISTS

That the mass market client relationship influences the actual books released by Global can be clearly seen in a comparison of the new title lists from Global and R&A. For example, certain expectable differences are clearly evident between the firms' spring 1974 and fall 1975 lists. In chapter 2 it was reported that 28 R&A titles were released in the fall and 19 were released in the spring. In contrast, Global released 44 titles in the fall and only 4 in the spring. This extreme numerical imbalance is explained by the Global selectors' realization that store buyers are likely to order new books only before Christmas. Such a consideration is irrelevant to R&A, except for their easy readers.

Other noteworthy differences between the firms' lists are Global's lower prices—most of its books cost $3 or less, while most of R&A's cost between $5 and $6; Global's adherence to color in 70 percent of its titles, as opposed to 4 percent in R&A's titles; Global's broader range of fiction and nonfiction subjects; Global's higher percentage of fantasy titles (40% to 15%); and its higher percentage of titles with anthropomorphic characters (40% to none). The variances in color and price reflect those basic differences in market approach already discussed. The difference in subject range reflects how the perceived requirements by Global selectors, to provide buyers with a wide variety of track record formats and subjects, differs in consequence from the R&A selectors' denial of rigid guidelines in favor of a general concept of age-oriented balance. And the difference in fantasy and anthropomorphic characterization can be attributed to the cartoon characters from other media that the Global selectors said they prefer. It should also be noted that Global's lists are, predictably, skewed toward the lower age ranges, with 60 percent of the titles directed predominantly at children 6 years or younger; on the R&A lists, only 34 percent of the titles fit this description.

The striking differences between the lists produced by Global and R&A, and the evident incompatibility between their guidelines, brings up a question. Do any of the mass market publisher's titles successfully cross over to Metrosystem? Before answering, a fact should be noted: although Global's selectors rarely consider libraries in making decisions about lines and titles, the division does fit library bindings to a certain percentage of titles that the library promotion department feels might sell to school and public libraries. (This library binding raises the retail price by a little over one dollar.) Certain lines are automatically excluded from consideration for the library market because their formats are too fragile (pop-ups), self-destructive (cut-outs), or too unlike traditional books to be acceptable to librarians (board books). Interestingly, the promotion director observed that the principal cross-over buyers are school, rather than public librarians. She said that the former are less concerned than the latter with literary quality and more concerned with using the interests engendered by the presold books among children for remedial reading and vocabulary skills.

The library promotion department's screening procedure is reflected in the fact that only 29 of the division's approximately 50 books were received at Metrosystem's coordinating office. Of those 29, 11 (38%)

were given full acceptance status by the Book Selection Committee; 5 (17%) were accepted by the regional branch and the central branch only; and the rest (45%) were rejected. The acceptance record is only 4 points lower than R&A's, though the number of titles judged and accepted was quite a bit higher in the case of the library market firm.

While the full acceptance record of the two firms is comparable, Metrosystem's considerably lower outright rejection of R&A titles (28%) suggests that librarians have distinctly different attitudes toward the divisions' products. Recall that comments on acceptance and rejection of R&A books by Metrosystem reviewers emphasized the success or failure of the individual works as quality juvenile literature. Global books, in contrast, were designated full acceptance when they met the coordinating office's most minimal literary acceptance standards, admittedly because of presold characteristics that would likely draw children to the books and make them very popular. In this connection, it is interesting to note that of the 11 books accepted, 9 were nonfiction. Nonfiction is an area the head of book selection conceded is treated more leniently than fiction from a literary standpoint. Global's fiction titles were more likely to be thought of as having "stilted, blunt, monotonous sentences and cheap illustrations."

Also of interest is that the 9 accepted nonfiction titles were about sports, a subject librarians noted were eagerly sought for by middle-aged and older boys. A typical review noted that the title, part of a line from which several had been rejected for quality reasons, "is unexceptional but it should fill the demand. Typical sportswriting style." It might be added that the two Global works of fiction accepted were by a name author-illustrator who has been with the firm since Global's library-oriented market days and has been accepted by Metrosystem despite his somewhat cartoony drawings. That person's popularity and the librarians' perceived need for sports books help explain why 7 of the Global acceptances were bought by over 30 of the 51 branches. One picture book was purchased by all of them.

These several acceptances do not refute the finding—seen throughout this chapter—that the strictures of the library market are quite different from the strictures of the mass market. The client relationships in both markets have wide-ranging significance for the publishing firms. However, the specific consequences for each firm vary with its specific relationship. It stands to reason that differences will also be seen among the chosen distribution outlets of the mass market and library market; whether this reasoning holds up is a subject for the next chapter.

Chapter 6: The Mass Market
Distribution Outlet

The feasibility of examining two mass market distribution outlets for this study stems, to a large degree, from the extremely compact nature of their organizations and selection procedures. Unlike the chosen library market outlet, which was seen to have a complex, two-tiered selection process involving approximately 40 selectors, the chosen bookstore chain, Bookwell, and department store chain, Gregory's, have central buyers for most (in the department store, all) of the books placed on the shelves in their branches throughout the area served by Metrosystem.

In the bookstore chain, juvenile book selection is separate from adult book-buying. The firm, with over 400 stores around the country and 4 in the city under study, divides its stock into four categories administered by five buying departments—adult hardbound; adult paperbound; adult promotional materials (remainders and reprints); juveniles (including juvenile hardbound, paperbound, and remainders); and nonbook materials (such as bookmarks and cards). Each department has one or more buyers who are responsible to the firm's executive officers. The Children's Book Department is comprised of a buyer and his assistant who review all new children's books and decide which should be introduced to the chain. They compile a semiannual check-list for all hardbacks and determine, with the help of computerized sales information, how many of each title should be sent to each store. New paperbacks are also reviewed by the buyers and ordered centrally, as are some extremely popular backlist titles. However, most backlisted paperbacks, because of their smaller number and because some branches might decide to allocate more wall space than others for their juveniles, are ordered by the individual stores with the aid of an initial stock title list distributed by the central office.

In the four locations of the outlets investigated for this study, the paperback ordering activity is carried out by an interested clerk, appointed by the store manager, who also racks incoming children's books and cares for their section's presentability. If customer demand warrants, store clerks are allowed, with the approval of the manager, to purchase hardbacks not on the checklist. Too much indulgence in this activity is frowned upon, however, since it undermines the firm's aim of getting maximum discount from the publishers through the large quantity purchases that accompany centralized ordering. More acceptable is the store clerk's advising the central buyer to send more or less than the computer-assigned quota of a particular title, depending on an individual estimation of the popularity of that title.

The department store's clerks have no responsibility at all for the juvenile books. Gregory's, a large, moderately priced chain that sells everything from gardening tools to clothes, employs one buyer to purchase and stock adult and juvenile books for the main store and its 10 branches throughout the city. Like Bookwell's buyers, the chain store buyer is responsible to the executive officers of the firm.

The purpose of this chapter is to explore the influence of their major clients upon the selection procedures of these two distribution outlet organizations. In view of the patterns that have been identified thus far, it should not be surprising to find that the same client relationship dynamic seen in the library system can also be seen with respect to Bookwell and Gregory's, albeit with different particulars reflecting the different market philosophies. In other words, similar approaches by the buyers in their interaction with publishers can be seen to operate in both outlet firms, approaches that tend to reinforce the prevailing selection perspectives and the power of already dominant firms. At the same time, the particulars embodied in these approaches are very different from those seen in Metrosystem, since the major client relationships are so very different. In this connection, although some differences in organizational requirements (and thus in existing guidelines) exist between the chosen mass market outlet organizations, the similarities are far more visible and important than the variances, and underscore the differences between the mass market and the library market.

THE BOOK SELECTION PROCEDURE

One difference between Metrosystem's selectors and selectors for Bookwell and Gregory's is that while the library market respondents had some perception of the influence maintained by the publishing firms of their segment upon their choice of books, the buyers from the two mass market organizations generally considered themselves quite autonomous from their suppliers regarding selection. The chief buyers stressed, in their interviews, that they, not the publishers' representatives (the salespeople), make all the decisions regarding the books that their stores will or will not buy. Nevertheless, as in Metrosystem, the buyers' answers to the interview questions reveal implicit approaches to their major client relationship that guide their understanding of book selection. Also, those approaches to the client relationship can be best understood by examining the two considerations that shape the selection procedure—the perception of general requirements with regard to selection material, and the manner in which such material is introduced to the organization.

GENERAL SELECTION REQUIREMENTS

Another similarity between the library market outlet and the mass market outlets regarding the influence of the client relationship should be noted. While interaction with publishers does not dictate the primary selection requirements, the relationship does reinforce a perspective that directs buyers towards fulfillment of those requirements in ways that strengthen the ties between them. Differing perceptions of organizational requirements lead the chief buyers of the department and bookstore chains to perceive this guiding perspective in slightly different manners and, consequently, they hold different attitudes towards the need for innovations in selection. Therefore, their approaches to children's books will be discussed separately.

The Chief Bookstore Buyer

The primary source of information about children's book selection in Bookwell was the chief juvenile buyer. With an assistant, unavailable for interview, he constantly deals with salespeople from different publishing firms and selects the books that are found in the juvenile department of every Bookwell store. In contrast, the five interviewed store clerks, primarily responsible for paperbacks, said that they have little contact with salespeople. Only two said that they had been visited by publishers' representatives during the past year, and even those clerks admitted such interactions are infrequent.

The centralized buying procedure was, according to the chief buyer, a fundamental organizational requirement; much of the success of the bookstore chain is based upon it. Centralized buying allows the firm to demand the maximum discount for every book it purchases, thus guaranteeing the highest possible profit margin per book. In order to guarantee the largest possible browsing traffic, the majority of bookstores have been located in malls.

Space for different product categories in each of the Bookwell stores, which are always the same size, is also allocated centrally, according to the firm's overall sales figures for those categories. Children's books, which ordinarily account for about 10 percent of the store sales, thus account for about 10 percent of the floor rack ("gondola") space plus the wall rack space around it, which may vary. This approximate 10 percent maximum places a limit on the number of books the juvenile buyer can assign to his section, and often makes the introduction of new books necessarily coincident with the excision of others. With space at a premium, each title placed in the juvenile area must be justified in terms of its ultimate profitability. This justification is carried out by noting or projecting the salability of a title (the frequency in which its stock turns) in relation to its per unit profit and the cost of the gondola or wall rack space it occupies. The buyer refused to reveal his usual turn requirement, but noted that he can be somewhat more lenient than adult book buyers because of the somewhat higher discount received on most children's books.

The Client Relationship

The children's buyer noted that the organizational requirements that have been described for his department are applicable to the other departments as well. However, he pointed out that while adult trade and paperback titles are bought in anticipation—or as a result—of advertising and publicity supporting them, with advertising costs sometimes shared by the publishers and the chain, children's books are expected to sell themselves without any such help.[1] The buyer seemed to accept the dearth of children's book promotion by publishers and the ignorance of store clerks on the subject of children's books as traditional factors to be taken into account, rather than as factors to be changed through a concerted effort of both publishers and outlets. The influence of the major client relationship is clearly evident in this attitude, which is not mandated by any particular Bookwell requirement. In view of the approaches used by the buyer's major—and most successful—suppliers, the mass market perspective simply represents the path of least resistance.

Of course, this path of least resistance continues to direct the buyer towards those firms that reinforce the validity of the perspective, those firms that in hardback and paperback have a track record of supplying books that sell themselves. Moreover, dependence on the line concept as an aid to achieving this goal helps further solidify these firms' dominant positions, since it is quite expensive and risky for a publisher without a mass market track record to create a line of books for that arena. An additional barrier to entry was indicated when the buyer noted that lines currently in the stores are only dropped for good reason, mainly if their sales begin to drop.

The Bookwell buyer did insist, however, that he is quite eager to place new titles, even new lines, in his store if he feels that they will help increase the sales figures of his department. He mentioned that mass market juvenile firms often solicit his advice with regard to particular subjects they are planning to publish, or new lines they want to create. The buyer said he usually hesitates to give advice on subjects for fear that the firms will start sending him manuscripts to read. He is eager, however, to advise publishing companies on lines they are considering. In unusual circumstances, if he really likes an idea, he said he might even guarantee the purchase of a group of books before publication. More often, he said that he might agree to test a new line in 25 stores to determine if its popularity warrants introduction throughout the chain.

Global Publishing's paperback picturebook line is particularly interesting in this connection. As noted in the previous chapter, the mass market publishing company has tied hopes for success of its small books on the spinner racks it supplies. The use of such racks is generally prohibited by Bookwell policy because their introduction on a large scale would either force the reduction of general gondola space or block aisles in violation of fire regulations. However, the Global salesperson convinced the buyer to test the books on the publisher-supplied equipment. The test produced excellent results—all racked books were sold out in three months. So, at the time of the interview, the buyer was petitioning his bosses for permission to use the Global spinner racks. It seems that in this unusual situation no books will have to be withdrawn if the pictureback line is accepted.

The Department Store Buyer

The requirements articulated by the Gregory's buyer regarding his work were similar to those of the Bookwell buyer. Limited space mandates a turnover in books that justifies the value of the space they occupy. Because the space allocated to his department varies in the different branches with the size of the branch store and the management's opinion of the book department's value, the buyer must stock the different stores with different quantities of children's books. Like the bookstore buyer, Gregory's buyer refused to state the minimum number of turns required by a typical juvenile book to maintain its berth on the department store racks. He did say, however, that while he examines the adult best sellers every week to project the number that will be needed in every store, he does not conduct this activity in the children's book area, since there are no hits. In the case of children's books and the other stock titles of the collection, he examines the sales figures cursorily every six weeks to pull the titles that have hardly moved at all. Every twelve weeks he surveys the collection more closely to delete books that have not been selling well enough and to augment titles or lines that have exceeded expectations.

Like the Bookwell buyer, the department store buyer implicitly approached the fulfilling of these organizational requirements with a basic acceptance of the traditional mass market rules of the game regarding juveniles—little, if any, advertising, and the choosing of titles primarily from firms that have shown that they can produce books that sell themselves. Unlike his bookstore counterpart, however, the buyer articulated a general indifference to new titles and formats in the juvenile book area, even within a mass market perspective. He stressed several times during the interview that all the department stores in town carry the same juvenile titles and that the same books always sell; hence, he feels no need to change his stock either in response to fashion or competition.

When asked whether he has bought the Global picturebooks, Gregory's buyer shrugged and said that he had initially bought some, but did not continue. He explained that since his department store's policy prohibits the use of promotional racks from publishers for aesthetic reasons, rather than because of fire regulations, he placed titles from the line with other juveniles on the store racks; when they failed to sell he returned them to the publishing house. Although the circumstances surrounding this situation might be considered unusual because of the firm's policy against racks, the buyer's lack of enthusiasm or interest for this new line, as compared to the interest of the bookstore buyer, is reflective of a general difference in their attitudes regarding innovation.

A large part of this difference seems to stem from the fact that while juvenile books comprise the bookstore buyer's entire purchasing domain, with his value to the company indicated by his ability to increase the juvenile category's percentage of total sales, the department store buyer is responsible for the bookstore as a whole and sees the adult area—the area of greatest movement and highest profit—as deserving the most intense concentration. In fact, Gregory's buyer could not even say what percentage of space or books in any store is devoted to children. He indicated that he has simply kept approximately the same floor space for children's books that he found when joining the firm three years ago.

HOW MATERIAL IS INTRODUCED

The preceding material has indicated how the influence of the mass market client relationship serves to illuminate and reinforce a mass market perspective for the book and department store buyers to follow in their conceptualizations of selection requirements. Remarks by the two chief buyers indicated that the dominance of the major client relationship—and the approach to books that it influences—is also reinforced through the manner in which books are introduced to the organization. Interestingly, this reinforcement seems to derive indirectly from library market firms, as well as directly from mass market publishing companies. Both buyers noted that salespeople representing firms that publish for school and public libraries, and whose primary aims are to sell adult titles to the book and department store chains, expect they will not sell their children's books, and so do not pitch their wares or do so only half-heartedly. Although both buyers pointed out that the salespeople are generally correct in this expectation, it seems clear that a cumulative consequence of this self-inhibition is to open the field for the mass market publishers' representatives, perpetuate the correctness of the mass market perspective in the eyes of the buyers, and aid in the continued dependence of the stores upon four or five firms for the bulk of their children's titles.

It should be added, however, that these firms do not supply the chain and bookstore buyers with the relatively small number of library market paperbacks that both distribution outlets carry. As previously noted, it was largely through the efforts of Dell, a large publisher of adult mass market paperbacks, that such books, primarily aimed at the adolescent and preadolescent, were accepted. R&A was very successful at following Dell's path. However, most library market children's book firms were unable to maintain the sales organizations needed to make the publication of paperbacks financially feasible. This was an invitation to four other large paperback firms to enter the children's book arena by buying subsidiary rights to popular library books and selling them to library, school, book fair, and commercial outlets, with libraries being the principal market.

The involvement of these paperback firms with children's books might bring about competition for the still-dominant mass market firms if the paperback firms expand successfully into the picture book and easy readers areas, where the bulk of children's sales resides. At present, however, the chain and department store buyers do not seem to see the library market paperbacks as being in competition with the products of the juvenile mass market firms. That the buyers tend to view those paperbacks as augmenting children's book sales is supported by the bookstore chain's separate ordering procedures for hardbacks and paperbacks. It is interesting to note that a few of the juvenile mass market firms, including Global, have already begun to capitalize on the now-accepted paperback format—for picture book lines and activity books. An example of the ability of these firms to maintain their dominance through the manner in which books are introduced can be seen in the fact that while the great proportion of library market paperbacks must be purchased by the clerks of individual stores, the mass market publishers' paperbacks are purchased centrally for all Bookwell stores. The central purchasing approach virtually assures a larger order.

DEPENDENCE AND INNOVATION IN STORE CHAINS

Although the department store buyer seemed quite satisfied with the products he buys from a small number of firms, his bookstore counterpart was annoyed with certain aspects of price and format which, he said, sometimes hinder him from deriving maximum benefit from his limited children's book space. For example, he accused one mass market firm of raising its prices under the guise of inflation merely to increase profits. He said that the importance of that company virtually forces him to buy its books, although he predicted that the higher prices will ultimately hurt the publishing house by slowing title movement and causing him to cut back on the purchasing of its books.

The buyer also noted that juvenile publishers, following Western Publishing, have been producing large-sized picture books in attempts to achieve more impact from book covers than their competitors and to crowd them off the shelves. He remarked that if all children's picture books were somewhat smaller in size, they would still sell well and the buyer would be able to stock more books in his children's book area. In another complaint about size, the buyer pointed out that trade-sized adolescent paperbacks, such as those produced by Dell and R&A, occupy the space of about two mass market paperbacks and thus reduce the number of books the store can carry. Consequently, in order to justify placing a $1.95 juvenile trade paperback on a wall rack, he has to be sure it will turn twice as quickly as two $1.95 juvenile paperbacks in the mass market format—a tough requirement.

The Bookwell buyer's interest in innovations that will help him expand the sales of his juveniles and his annoyance at some aspects of his major suppliers' products has led him to be more eager than the department store buyer to consider the products of nondominant firms that conform to the mass market perspective. The acceptance of titles from such firms is, however, not common, both because relatively few firms attempt to compete in the mass market arena and because the buyer tends to make room for new lines only when a significant reduction in the sales of an already entrenched line is occurring. One case in which a line was partially dropped in order to make room for another of a nondominat firm dealt, interestingly, with the Global and R&A easy readers. The buyer said that visits to branches, reports from store managers, and computerized sales records

101

showed him that Global's easy readers, which had until then been the sole easy reader line the store carried, had begun to drop quite strongly and consistently. Reasoning that perhaps he should introduce another easy reader line, the buyer tested one firm's titles for several months, with mediocre results. Rejecting those, he then tried R&A's competitively priced easy readers. They have sold quite well, and the buyer has reduced his purchases of the Global titles to make room for the other line. It might be noted that, consistent with the differences regarding innovations that have been drawn between the book and department store buyers, Gregory's buyer has not even experimented with the R&A easy readers in his stores.

The differences in book selection requirements between the bookstore and department store buyers have been traced to their differing perceptions of their organizational responsibilities. In addition, the major client relationship has operated in both cases to reinforce the mass market perspective while discouraging the buyers from considering—and encouraging suppliers to consider—alternative approaches. The final sections of this chapter will illustrate how locking into the mass market client relationship—and into the perspective that it shapes—has ramifications for the buyers' images of their audience, their guidelines of selection, and the actual new books that they purchase.

CLIENT RELATIONSHIP AND AUDIENCE IMAGE

The mass market perspective's injunction to supply books that sell themselves carries with it an implicit assumption about the audience as generally uninformed about juveniles, and consequently interested only in superficial aspects of the displayed titles. The chief buyers for Bookwell and Gregory's indicated their acceptance of this assumption, though they freely admitted that they really know very little about the people who purchase juvenile books in their stores. The buyers and the Bookwell clerks did contribute to the impression that while many juveniles are bought as gifts by parents or grandparents when children are not present, many books are also purchased by adults accompanied by children. One clerk pointed out that the juvenile section is usually placed at the rear of a Bookwell store and that children are often sent there by their parents to play and look at books while their parents browse; children's book purchases often result from this activity. The clerk also echoed the other mass market outlet respondents in saying that adolescents are likely to choose and pay for books themselves.

These same notions about relative parent-child participation in choosing books from mass market outlet shelves were also articulated by the Global selectors. The comments by librarians about the parental role in selecting titles for young children from the library shelves were different—reflecting librarian participation and somewhat greater child autonomy—but not drastically so. At striking variance with the comments of branch librarians, however, were the remarks by both chief buyers that they are not concerned with characteristics of particular neighborhoods when selecting books. The buyers noted that such considerations are irrelevant, since their stores are generally located in large shopping districts or malls that are frequented by people from different areas of the city. Two of the bookstore clerks interviewed did, however, attempt to stock some supplementary juveniles aimed at particular groups living in the local community.

Responding to a question about audience characteristics, two clerks stated that it was their impression that a large percentage of the juvenile book purchasers are well off in terms of income and education. This speculation, echoed by a few people from mass market publishing firms other than Global, cannot be strictly compared to the survey findings that librarians in middle class areas where children have excellent reading abilities, who tend to feel that parents who visit their branches know a lot about children's books. Nevertheless, such a comparison does suggest a possible clash between these librarians' opinions and the mass market presumption that the audience generally has little sophistication with regard to children's books. At any rate, the clerks' view of their main audience's socioeconomic status had the same negative affect on them as it had on publishing selectors: it justified their general refusal to accept titles set in deprived areas or having children of minority races as main characters.

BOOK SELECTION GUIDELINES

Espousal of the mass market perspective's fundamental assumption about audience knowledgeability regarding children's books could also be seen to have ramifications for the guidelines that the chief buyers adopted for the titles they purchase. Not surprisingly, both buyers set forth the same two criteria that the Global selectors expressed for choosing material that sells itself—low price and track record.

Low price meant books from about 95¢ to $4.95 for Gregory's or $5.95 for Bookwell. The bookstore buyer noted that a 69¢ line was rejected because it would not pay for its space even according to the most optimistic estimation of its turn frequency. He refused to see the importance of price in relative, competitive terms. He insisted that people are extremely price sensitive in the case of juveniles: if prices rise, they simply stop buying as many books. The department store buyer noted that remainders, which are very low-priced (usually somewhat over $1), are popular sellers in the children's area because people feel that one children's book is as good as another; consequently, price is their distinguishing characteristic.

As for track record, the buyers emphasized the importance of a publishing house's previous success (a self-perpetuating aspect of the client relationship) and the presold nature of the books in terms of line, character identifiability, author, illustrator, or subject. With regard to these areas, a remarkable similarity exists between the guidelines of the outlet selectors and those of the mass market publishing selectors. Books for preschool and early grade children were noted as most popular. Full color was deemed essential for picture books; the bookstore buyer said that customers choose full-color books over others, and that as long as some companies turn out full color at low prices these will get priority on the racks. Both buyers were also fond of adolescent series books since, if popular, they can be racked spine out and still sell. Interestingly, the book store buyer confirmed a Global editor's observation that the sales of hardback juvenile sports books are on the decline, because children have been buying adult sports paperbacks.

The buyers also noted that cover art and illustrations are very important in the evaluation of most juveniles, but neither could articulate the criteria used to judge these areas. The department store buyer pointed to picture books with Walt Disney characters and illustrations as examples of books that always move well. The bookstore buyer, when asked to specify his preferences regarding illustrations, said "I don't play critic" and pointed to two new, brightly illustrated titles that he had recently selected. Similarity to previously successful titles seemed to be the implicit criterion, along with a reliance on the judgment of the successful mass market publisher.

Crossovers from the Library Market

Both buyers pointed out that they carry some books that were originally intended for school and public libraries. The department store buyer characterized these more expensive titles as gift books; he stocks these with a collection of hardbound classics, such as *Little Women* and *Heidi,* purchased from a mass market publishing firm. The buyer said that he purchases very few library market titles; he only picks them up if it is clear that they will have an audience. For example, he mentioned ordering Maurice Sendak's *In the Night Kitchen* after it was highlighted on the "60 Minutes" television program because of a controversy among librarians and parents surrounding an illustration of a naked child. The buyer noted

104

that most gift books are only placed in the chain's main store. The more limited space of the branch departments precludes the introduction of all but the books that will sell most quickly and profitably. Different price points do seem to do better at different branches, he said.

The bookstore buyer, with a larger, more permanent collection of these titles in each store, also spoke of their sales as gifts and said that the titles are purchased after they have won awards or have achieved a large following in libraries. A clerk said that she might order a title if customers who have seen a newspaper article or "Today" show review request it. Note that these library market titles—including picture books—are generally racked spine out in the stores, making it necessary for them to be sought out or discovered, and preventing them from selling themselves most effectively. Another interesting point is that most of the library market books bought are from firms having extensive dealings in the adult area; R&A is one of these.

Library Market Paperbacks. Library market paperbacks are somewhat different from the library market hardbacks or the mass market children's books, since they are essentially promoted by librarians, teachers, and institutional book clubs among the mostly adolescent or preadolescent children who buy them. The Bookwell and Gregory's chief buyers indicated that children's paperbacks, usually novels, are chosen for indications of presold popularity—either because they are immediately recognizable classics, because they relate to films or television shows, or because they have recently become very popular in the library and/or institutional book club spheres. The department store buyer said that he carries several R&A paperbacks that have been adapted for other mass media, a group of classic Dell paperbacks, and scattered titles from other firms—most in trade format. The four Bookwell clerks who were interviewed pointed to larger paperback sections with both mass market and trade sized titles.

It is important to note that three of the four clerks who order most of the paperbacks for the outlets studied did not seem to have a wide knowledge of the children's book field. Although they claimed an interest in the area, their knowledge of hardback titles and authors seemed generally to be confined to the books that their stores receive through the central buying process. Since the library market hardbacks that are turned into paperbacks do not, in the great majority of cases, appear in bookstores, the buyers are not familiar with the titles on the publishers' paperback lists. Ordering paperbacks, therefore, is generally done by choosing from among the stocked books that sold best when the clerks started working, by picking authors who have track records in other paperbacks, and by responding to children and teachers who occasionally ask for certain titles.

In striking contrast to the librarians, the three clerks admitted that they

105

do not read the paperbacks that they buy and often do not know what kind of books they are really getting until they arrive. None of them could remember any controversies generated by the sale of popular new realism titles by Judy Blume, Norma Klein, and others in paperback. One said she tries to screen the incoming books for objectionable titles, but noted that her lack of knowledge about their content makes this task difficult.

The knowledgeable exception among the clerks was a former elementary school teacher who has been purchasing paperbacks in consultation with teachers in the area who want to assign them to students. She said that the store's manager allows her to keep a paperback section quite a bit larger than most, even though its sales are not commensurate with its size. The clerk also noted that in response to complaints that the children's books in her store do not include minority group members as main characters, she deviated from the hardback check list and bought several books about black, Puerto Rican, and Chinese children. Like the juvenile titles in the store, the books were simply placed on the racks and expected to sell themselves. They did not turn adequately, however, and, after several months the clerk removed them.

The initiative, knowledgeability, and deliberate community orientation displayed by the former schoolteacher in her paperback and hardback purchases was, as noted, an exception to the other clerks and, more important, to the Gregory's and Bookwell buyers. Their guidelines and activities reflected the mass market perspective clearly and thoroughly. How that perspective has consequences for the actual books presented to store customers will be discussed in the remainder of this chapter.

THE CLIENT RELATIONSHIP AND THE SEASONAL LISTS

The book lists to be discussed here belong to only one of the mass market outlets, Bookwell. Unfortunately, new book lists could not be obtained from Gregory's buyer. It is also unfortunate that the Bookwell lists include only hardbacks. Whereas an analysis of the library's new hardbacks could be said to cover all new books, since all paperbacks were originally purchased in hardback, such a statement cannot be made about either the book or department store chains. In order to chart the impact of paperbacks on the Bookwell customer's spectrum of choice, the juvenile paperback rack in a representative Bookwell store was audited; of course, the rack included both new and old titles. With regard to the department store, an impressionistic but lengthy examination of the children's books in stock indicated that it was much like Bookwell's. However, consistent with the preceding discussion, Gregory's collection was somewhat smaller in the main store (much smaller in the branches), with fewer new titles and a main store paperback rack holding only half the titles found in the audited Bookwell rack.

Perhaps the most important discovery made in the comparison of Bookwell's list and Global Publishing's list is that there is a close correspondence between the two organizations in terms of categories accepted. Recall that when the outputs of R&A and Metrosystem were compared, the rather narrow scope of the library market publisher's titles was seen as further evidence that the library market client relationship supports firms that publish according to editor preference—as long as they choose good books. The Global-Bookwell comparison shows that the mass market client relationship has a different influence: it causes the publishing selectors to select a very similar spectrum of titles.

An examination of the number of new titles that Bookwell's buyer purchased from publishers further illustrates the role of the mass market client relationship in influencing the spectrum of choice for the ultimate audience. Of the 54 new titles accepted by Bookwell, all in the fall, 53 (98%) were from the three largest mass market publishers, and Global was among these. Interestingly, the one library market book bought was from a Global subsidiary. In regard to Global itself, Bookwell accepted 20 (55%) of the 45 titles (29 fall and 16 spring) that the publisher released during the fall 1975 and spring 1976 seasons. Note that this acceptance rate was higher than the firm's 38 percent acceptance in Metrosystem. Moreover, 16 of the 25 rejections can be seen as automatic in view of the buyers' evident refusal to purchase new titles in the spring, the non-Christmas season. When compared to Metrosystem's acceptance of a small percentage of new mass market books, Bookwell's rejection of all but one library market title supports the idea that the mass market client relationship leads outlet selectors to be less flexible and more dependent upon the segment's dominant producers than does the library market client relationship.

Dominance by the three mass market children's publishers was lessened somewhat by the presence of paperbacks in the Bookwell stores on wall racks titled "Young Readers." Even here, however, the presold dictum of the mass market perspective could be seen. In the representative store that was audited, 105 nonpicture book paperback titles were found—62 in mass market paperback format and 43 in trade size, the former usually being for somewhat older readers. Only 9 (8%) of the 105 were paperback originals; all those were in mass market format and had presold character identifiability because of tie-ins to television programs ("The

Waltons," for example) or Disney films. Moreover, only 42 of the 105 (40%) were actually derived from contemporary library market hardback titles.

Aside from the paperback originals, the remaining 62 paperbacks in the mass market format were either instantly recognizable classics (such as *National Velvet* and *Little House on the Prairie*) or, in somewhat lesser numbers—25 (40%)—sure-fire library market romances or new realism titles like those by Judy Blume or Norma Klein. The 43 trade paperbacks consisted of 26 classics (60%), with the rest being very popular contemporary library market titles. Ironically, then, the only paperbacks not in the store because they could sell themselves as classics or as tie-ins from other mass media were those produced, accepted, and promoted as a result of the usually incompatible library market client relationship.

COMPARISON OF THE METROSYSTEM
AND BOOKWELL SELECTIONS

Perhaps it should be stressed that the paperback audit just presented is an audit of all titles in a representative store, not just of titles received for the first time. Because of the important absence of paperbacks in the analysis of new books selected by Bookwell, it is strictly inappropriate to compare the new books accepted by the chain with the new books accepted by Metrosystem, which does not accept new titles in paperback. However, some differences may be discussed that would undoubtedly not be affected by the addition of paperbacks to the bookstore chain's lists. Immediately striking, for example, is the variance between the number of titles accepted by Metrosystem (925) and those selected by Bookwell (54). The difference is obviously partially due to the much more limited amount of space in the bookstores as compared to the library, and partly to the manner in which the books are released to the ultimate audience: in the library the same book will be circulated and returned, while in the bookstore it will be removed permanently and replaced by another copy.

The difference in selection between the two outlets does not end with the number of titles bought, however. Other differences include Metrosystem's much greater variety and percentage (49% to 27%) of nonfiction titles, as well as Metrosystem's smaller percentage of picture books (12% to 52%). As might be predicted from previous discussions of these outlets, the selection differences reflect both differences in the organizations' requirements and the different influences of their major client relationship. The librarians' perceived organizational requirement to select nonfiction to help children with school assignments accounts for the difference in nonfiction purchases. In Bookwell, adherence to the mass market perspective locks the buyers into a smaller spectrum of proven areas like sports, monsters, magic, and automobiles. Of course, the bookstore buyers and librarians are ultimately dependent upon the books their market's producers publish for them. As has been seen, the library market encourages proliferation of many more firms and, thus, a wider spectrum of choice within the good books perspective than does the mass market.

This two-directional influence of the client relationships with respect to outlets and production organizations also explains the small percentage of picture books found in Metrosystem compared to Bookwell. Librarians did not say anything negative about picture books; on the contrary, they welcomed them as books easy to circulate. However, the high costs of producing picture books and the uncertainty over any particular title's marketability have led many publishers to take advantage of the libraries' acceptance of other types of books. They have turned, particularly, to curriculum-oriented nonfiction that might also be bought by schools for classroom use. The mass market publishers, in contrast, have a more captive market in their outlets and can thus more reliably guide the success of their picture books.

Other variances between the outlets that reflect the different impacts of their client relationships are Bookwell's lower prices (under $4 for most books against $6 in the library), Bookwell's higher percentage of titles with anthropomorphic characters (55% to 6%), and Bookwell's larger variety of formats in books for young children (4 to 2). While these differences are sufficient to point out the differential influence of the client relationships, they cannot uncover the myriad incompatibilities in content and production values that have kept the two segments separate. At various points in this book, examinations of the selection requirements and guidelines of selectors have contributed to understanding these compatibilities. In the process, the examinations have chronicled the crucial importance of the library market and mass market client relationships to the separation of the two segments and to the drastically different approaches to children's books at both the production and distribution levels.

Chapter 7: Summary and Analysis

The two-directional influence of the client relationship that has been discussed in the preceding pages has only been observed clearly in the organizations that were scrutinized for this study. However, interviews with personnel from several mass market and library market firms have suggested quite strongly that the influences described in this work can be seen in the other organizations within the segments as well. Moreover, it is possible that the production and distribution dynamics shown as operating in both segments in this case study might be generalized beyond children's book publishing to other mass media complexes.

The purpose of this final chapter is to discuss these possibilities. First, a general analytic framework will be presented to summarize and explain the findings. Then, the utility of this framework for understanding and predicting the activity of mass media organizations will be suggested. Some attention will be paid to the use of the idea of client relationship for research on mass media complexes in general; the American children's television complex, in particular, will be discussed. However, the greatest interest will be placed on the implications of client relationships for the production and distribution of children's books and, ultimately, for the children who read them.

THE CLIENT RELATIONSHIP AS A COMMUNICATION SYSTEM

Certain words that recur throughout this study—"two-directional," "systemic," "interaction"—indicate that the key to understanding the influence of the client relationship may lie in conceiving it as a communication system involving the patron and production organizations of the mass media complex. The function of such a communication system for each organization in the relationship is suggested by a prominent body of material on the sociology of work that stresses the importance of routinizing tasks in organizations to allow control of work.[1] Routinization assumes—indeed requires—at least a minimum level of predictability with regard to aspects of the organization's environment essential to the organization's success. Therefore, it can be seen that one important goal of an organization would be to achieve a predictability level with respect to its environment, one that would maximize the profitability of routines. Such a goal, it can be suggested, would lead an organization to try to coordinate its activities with those of extraorganizational entities relevant to its success while, at the same time, attempting to exert as much control as possible over the activities of those relevant entities.

Although the routinization of activities by selectors in Global Publishing, R&A Publishing, Gregory's, Bookwell, and Metrosystem has not been a major theme of this work, the idea that they engage in relatively predictable patterns of operation has been implicit throughout. The discussions of book selection activities and guidelines imply that members of each organization have patterned approaches to their work. A comparison of responsibilities and freedoms held by selectors in publishing firms, moreover, reveals that the degree of routinization varies: the library market's publishing firm is low in routine procedures compared to its mass market counterpart.

In view of the necessity for stable organizational operations, it is significant that the client relationship—and the production and distribution dynamics that characterize it—has been seen in this study as the primary factor that initially shapes and subsequently perpetuates the patterned activities of the patron and production organizations in each segment. The crucial influence of the client relationship upon these processes derives from the continuous patron-production interactions that make up the relationship: those interactions make up a communication system through which the requirements and opportunities of each member with regard to its counterpart in the relationship can be perceived, understood, and acted upon.

With respect to shaping organizational activities, the client relationship has been seen as the source of historical and functional explanations regarding the existence of particular structures and processes in the organizations that were examined. In both cases, the publishing firms' continual interactions with outlets and consequent conceptions of client relationship have influenced the structure of decision making; the processes of selecting books to be published; the guidelines for selecting content characteristics; the images of the people who read the books; and the types of books actually published. Moreover, the differences in client relationship were found to explain consistent differences of structure and process in the two organizations. Appropriately responding to demands and opportunities of

111

its library market clients, R&A Publishing was loosely compartmentalized, with its selectors low in routine activities as compared to Global Publishing. Global, for its part, found a more rigid approach as an appropriate response to its continual interaction with mass market outlets. The differences in organizational routine might relate to differences in the aesthetic orientation of the client relationship: in the library market client relationship aesthetic considerations are foremost, while in the mass market they are not. It might be that high attention to aesthetic guidelines demands a looser production structure and routine.

A rather broad influence is exerted by publishers upon their distribution outlets. Although the outlets have general requirements that preceded their interactions with publishers, the different client relationships do influence the adoption of particular practices in each outlet. For example, the book review and selection process in Metrosystem is influenced by the library market publishers' custom of sending the System Coordinating Office complimentary copies of new books. Similarly, a general acceptance by the department and bookstore buyers of the notion that children's books should be visualized in lines, not as individual titles, relates to the buyers' continual interaction with representatives of mass market publishers over a long period of time.

The client relationship is also the instrument through which the outlets gain information about future publications. The most important outlet selectors collect announcements about books to be published so as to coordinate their buying plans with publishers' plans; they also attempt to influence the direction of publication. These activities are most clearly identified with the library coordinators and with the main bookstore buyer. However, even the department store buyer, who saw children's books as a fairly minor area of his work, was quite conscious that in following the path of least resistance and purchasing from only a few mass market firms, he was helping to perpetuate the production of the types of books most useful to his store.

Learning distributors' perceptions is essential for the success of the publishers in their areas of interest. Not only are the publishing selectors much more concerned than the outlets with receiving feedback about their counterparts in the client relationship; they are also more concerned with using the client relationship to reinforce certain selection perspectives in the marketplace and to guide those counterparts in certain directions of children's literature. This difference can be traced to the extent that the publisher depends on outlets for survival. While the solvency of the publishing firms in both segments is directly dependent upon the continued patronage of their clients, the solvency of the clients (the distribution outlets) is not directly dependent upon the publishing firms. The need of the publishers

112

to maintain control over their outlets' selection perspectives can also be undertood in view of the fact that their routinized processes and their structures are based, to a much larger extent than those of the outlets, on demands of their partners in the client relationship. In other words, having organized their activities and power bases around the rules of that relationship, the producers are particularly determined to maintain their power by maintaining those rules. The client relationship/communication system helps them achieve this aim.

THE SIGNIFICANCE OF THE CLIENT RELATIONSHIP

One important finding of this study is that the manner in which a firm responds in its client relationship is, in large part, determined by the manner in which the firm's principal selectors conceptualize that relationship. Different perceptions of requirements and opportunities, based upon different perceptions of organizational demands and, in the case of publishing selectors, marketplace characteristics will necessarily lead to somewhat different approaches to book selection. This study's findings also imply, however, that client expectations tend to describe certain editorial boundaries that a firm cannot sidestep if it is to succeed in its chosen marketplace. Thus, the findings suggest that a comparison of firms from the same segment that have different personalities would yield greater similarities in structure, process, and product than would a comparison of firms from different segments.

To illustrate, the reader will recall that R&A's editors felt that their marketplace is very conducive to publishing the fiction titles they love. At the same time, the management of another prominent publishing division has also observed that market and stressed the relative ease by which nonfiction titles are chosen by public libraries—and the curriculum-oriented school libraries. Consequently, that firm's selectors have followed a tack very different from R&A's: they concentrate on releasing books librarians will buy to help children with schoolwork. It is very important to note, however, that despite this difference in approach from R&A, the publishing firm is much more similar in structure and process to R&A than to Global or any other firm in the mass market.

Generalizing these findings a bit more, it is interesting to relate the organizational processes in the two children's book segments to Arthur Stinchcombe's discussion of administrative styles in organizations.[2] Stinchcombe distinguishes between two such styles—bureaucratic and craft. The former, he says, "may be defined by the criterion that both the product and the work process are planned in advance by persons who are not of the

113

work crew"—that is, by managers in the organization. In craft administration, by contrast, all the characteristics of the work process are governed by specially hired workers "in accordance with the empirical lore that make up craft principles"; management only denotes specifications of the product desired. According to this terminology, the "work crew" of children's book production consists of the authors and illustrators, while the "managers" are the selectors. Tying these terms to the findings of this book, we can suggest that any mass media complex with a client relationship oriented primarily toward aesthetic goals, as is the library market client relationship, will encourage a generally craftlike administration of production. And, we can predict, a client relationship primarily oriented to nonaesthetic goals, as is the mass market relationship, will lead to a generally bureaucratic administration of production. Of course, research on other mass media complexes must be carried out to determine if these hypotheses can be supported.

This book's examination of library market and mass market client relationships has also cast new light upon the approaches of selectors toward their purported audience, children. This research tends to support previous conclusions that factors other than the ultimate audience are more immediately important to people who select mass media content, though impressions of the audience do play a significant role—and not always merely a background role. However, the findings of this study go beyond the others in revealing that the audience impressions that the selectors maintain are, to a large degree, actually transformed reflections of the spectra of choice the selectors helped establish and, at root, transformed reflections of their publishing perspectives. These perspectives are shaped by perceptions of organizational demands and opportunities which, in turn, are structured and/or reinforced by major client relationships. Not only does this situation hold true in the publishing firms and mass market outlets, where selectors admit to having very little, if any, information about their readers; it also obtains in the chosen library system, where selectors have first-hand information about the children. It is true that judgments of popularity (what sells and circulates) are important among all selectors as indicators of what the audience wants. However, such judgments are determined within the confines of options derived from existing audience images.

These observations regarding the audience highlight its abstract nature, as it refers to groups that are ultimate targets of messages. In theory, there is an infinite number of ways to look at the people who come into contact with mass media content; in this sense, there is an infinite number of audiences. Unfortunately, most writers in mass media organizations have tended to reify the concept of audience, to accept demographic or other data presented by those organizations as actually referring to the audience for that mass medium.[3] The suggestion here is that "audience" is a useful construct and should be viewed as such. Moreover, it is suggested that the audiences that are constructed (that is, the audience categories focused upon) by selectors within mass media patron and production organizations are influenced by the reward systems under which the patron selectors operate, are discovered and adopted by production selectors who want to be subsidized by those patrons, and are perpetuated by both sides of the client relationship because of compatible—though not congruent—interests.

SOME GENERALIZATIONS

Generalizing beyond children's book publishing, it can be suggested that the perspective on client relationship that has been developed in this work, along with a method for studying it, might have applicability to research on many mass media complexes. It should be noted, though, that while the patron organizations in the children's book industry are outlets, this situation does not hold in every mass media complex. In the American commercial broadcasting system, for example, advertisers are the patrons, while broadcasting companies that hold transmitting licenses are often the outlets, and network organizations are sometimes producers.

In view of the pervasiveness of television in America, it might be productive to compare briefly the client relationships noted in children's book publishing with those in children's television. Two types of client relationships dominate that field. In the commercial area, the three commercial television networks vie for orders from advertisers. The objectives of patrons and producers in the public television client relationship has always seemed primarily pedagogical—to lure children to the set in order to teach them elementary concepts and give them a head start in school. In commercial television, the objectives of patrons and producers are very different—to deliver a child audience to advertisers who want to convince the youngsters to buy (or nag their parents to buy) certain products.

The specific consequences of such patron-producer interactions for the creation and distribution of particular children's television content has not been investigated. However, Melody's[4] incisive analysis of the industry sheds a good deal of light on the client relationship in that area and points to the same general dynamics observed in the children's book field. Moreover, his discussion seems to bear out the earlier suggestion that a non-aesthetically based client relationship would result in highly routine and formulaic production activities. The assumptions and activities guiding the spectrum of choice among commercial television's children's program selectors appear, in some respects, to be similar to those observed in the mass market segment of children's book publishing. Emphasis is placed on low cost production techniques, presold characters, and the series concept. The television producers have, however, used the kinetic capability of television to forge an additional convention: their approach is to use action, often violent action, to keep children glued to their chairs for those all-important commercial minutes.

Public television's child programming has been hailed as a success in its objectives by many, though others have decried the narrowness of its goal and claimed undesired side effects.[4] Commercial children's television has been lambasted from many sides. Some critics have used the same charges leveled against mass market books—low aesthetic creativity, little awareness of varied child backgrounds and capabilities, too high fantasy orientation. Some have attacked the programs' violent content. Some have questioned the desirability of presenting advertising to children. Melody, who wants to reshape commercial television for children, has suggested "the development of a structure of separate decision-making entities to make programming decisions that reflect considerations of the needs and interests of children . . . in which problems related to basic commercial-system objectives . . . do not color program selection desires."[5] He does not elaborate on this proposal, but one way to carry it through would be to create a relationship between organizations producing children's shows and groups that select those shows that would resemble the aesthetically-based library market client relationship.

To some extent the ties between educational groups and the Public Broadcasting System probably already resemble the library market relationship. If this situation were desired on commercial television as well, implementation could proceed as follows: time slots currently used to program for children (or other preferred slots) would be partially or fully removed from network control by a Federal Communications Commission edict much like the "prime time access rule."[6] These periods would be returned to the local stations with the directive that they program children's fare. Advertising support would be allowed for such programming. However, advertising could not be placed in the middle of programs; nor would sponsors be allowed to choose the shows they want to precede or follow. Fixed commercial space would be allocated sequentially on a first-come, first-served basis.

During the designated children's time period, librarians specially trained in television and film arts would be hired by the local library system to comprise program selection committees. The purpose of these committees would be to use money from advertisers and any additional money available to rent programs from production firms. A fixed percentage of the advertising money above organizational costs would accrue as profit to the stations; the program selection committees would be delegated to spend the rest of all incoming cash on programs. Antitrust regulations would be relaxed; cooperation between several stations in the same area would be encouraged, thus allowing librarians at different stations to program blocks of time devoted to different types of children. If what has been learned about client relationships is generalizable, these changes in the patron organizations would result in very different interactions with production firms. The new interactions would bring about complementary changes in process, structure, audience image—and product—among the production firms.

Stability and Change

Generalizations about client relationship can also be useful in making tentative predictions about the children's book industry itself. It is interesting, for example, to speculate about what would occur if publishers from one of the segments studied tried to expand into the outlets of the other segment. Such speculation is not idle, since the precipitous loss of funds among many school and public libraries during the early 1970s has led to suggestions by editors that library market publishing firms lessen their dependence on libraries by increasing their attention to bookstores.[7] The analysis presented in this volume suggests that any such cross-overs of new titles could only be realistically attempted by large firms that have functioning trade apparatuses to help their children's imprints make the transition from one promotion environment to another. Even in such cases, however, the often incompatible differences between the mass market and library market perspectives on children's books would seem to dictate major changes in the types of books produced and, ultimately, in the manner in which they are produced. R&A's relatively standardized production of easy readers, while still a fairly peripheral activity for the division, is one example of the shift in organizational perspective that even a minor orientation towards the mass market will yield. The increased compartmentalization of book selection activities in Global Publishing as it veered more consciously toward the mass market a half decade ago is a further illustration that the decision to follow the orientation of another marketplace had ramifications for the entire production organization, ramifications which might yield titles incompatible with the previously held perspective.

Of course, another way to approach the problem might be to try to persuade the mass market outlets, particularly the bookstores, to adopt a library market perspective. Again, however, because the espousal of this

117

viewpoint has ramifications for an entire range of organizational activities, it would probably not be implemented, especially in view of the efficient and profitable nature of the dominant mass market client relationship. A buyer from a large bookstore chain (not Bookwell) did, in fact, dismiss the suggestion that his firm train clerks to, in effect, act as librarians and introduce children and parents to unfamiliar library market titles and authors. He said his firm pays clerks so little, and personnel turnover is so high, that the firm could not afford such specialists.

One way library market publishers might make their new titles more desirable to bookstores would be to advertise and promote them as they do their adult books, so as to presell them to children and children walking through the store. When asked about this possibility, interviewed subjects from the library market claimed lack of funds to adequately publicize such titles, and a bias by the popular reviewing channels against children's books that would take much effort to overcome. To simply exhort people to buy children's books, they noted, would only help the books already in the stores. These observations about the client relationship lead, then, to the conclusion that the separation between the two segments with regard to new titles (and most old ones, despite the increased sales of paperback reprints in the mass market) is bound to continue.

Linking Research on Book Distribution to Research on Effects

It is important to note that the discussion thus far has not concerned itself with the desirability of a separation or a mixing of the two segments. Indeed, the question of the consequences that books produced in the mass market and those produced in the library market have for the children who read them has barely been broached. "Consequences" in this case can be understood to cover a wide range of effects upon children who read the books—concept and vocabulary learning; expansion (or dimunition) of aesthetic sensibility and creativity; broadening (or narrowing) of world view and critical faculties; increasing (or decreasing) eagerness to read; and more. In addition, the fact that library market books are most often borrowed by or for the child while mass market books are most often bought raises the question of the psychological benefits of book possession as opposed to book borrowing—and the difference, if any, that mass market and library market books make in this regard.

These questions can be seen as closely complementing the findings of this work, since knowledge about the structure and operation of the complex that produces children's books can be joined to conclusions about the relative merit and desirability of different kinds of juveniles. Children's book editors and librarians are partners in the creation of quality in children's literature, but unfortunately much of their writing lacks a critical perspective that will allow the discussion of this issue on a plane removed from the biases of the library market. Disagreements usually revolve around issues such as censorship that do not challenge the range of fundamental assumptions held by selectors. Many of the articles are quite self-congratulatory in tone and imply that the sole goal—and ultimate influence—of all those connected with the production and distribution of children's books is to create a reading environment for the child that will be the source of "everlasting growth, wonder, and delight."[8]

More and more open public debate on children's books, stimulated by research on the organizations that produce them and the consequences they have for children, can lead to new insights and sophisticated blueprints for constructive change. This research approach—combining findings about the consequences of mass media content with understanding of the forces that operate to shape the content—should actually be carried out with regard to the entire spectrum of mass media that people encounter in their daily activities. It is only through a multifaceted approach to mass media research that a society can ever hope to reshape and redirect the messages that comprise a large part of its symbolic environment.

119

Appendix: Survey Procedures Used

The purpose of this appendix is to allow the interested reader more detail concerning the manner in which the investigation discussed in this book was carried out. As mentioned in the Introduction, the focus of a large part of the research was on those positions in each organization that have responsibility for determining the books to be accepted. People in such positions can be designated as production or outlet selectors, depending on whether they belong to production or outlet organizations in the segment.

Two types of selectors in each organization can be usefully defined. A *direct selector* is one who has direct power over the selection, timing, withholdng, or repetition of particular messages. An *indirect selector* is one who controls the resources, information or money, that are needed by direct selectors in order for them to perform their duties. For example, children's book editors are usually direct selectors, while children's book salespeople and promotion people, who inform the editors of the types of books sought by outlets, are usually indirect selectors.

Figure 1 presents a schematic diagram of the research design and notes the direct and indirect selectors contacted. The objective was to reach all direct selectors in each organization. The number of direct selectors in the publishing firms of both segments and in the mass market distribution outlet organizations was small enough so that an attempt could be made to interview all of them. However, the large number of librarians (45) necessitated the distribution of survey questionnaires to them after a one-third sample was interviewed. It was also decided that key indirect selectors who were mentioned by direct selectors in their interviews should be approached, since their input might be crucial to selection decisions. These selectors were especially prominent in the publishing firms; interviews with them, as well as with a small number of salespeople (most of whom worked in the outlets' cities) were carried out.

Figure 1. Schematic Diagram of Research in Focal Organizations

LIBRARY MARKET   MASS MARKET

PRODUCERS

Library Market Publishing Firm

The juvenile division's publisher*
3 senior editors*
2 of 4 associate editors*
1 of 3 readers*
The firm's vice president (vp)
  for finance
The firm's vp for marketing
The juvenile marketing director
The juvenile/adult library promotion
  and advertising director
The juvenile/adult publicity director
The paperback division's sales
  director
The assistant production manager
  (juvenile)
The firm's director of foreign rights
The juvenile division's director of
  subsidiary rights
4 of 19 trade salespeople
1 of 7 paperback salespeople

Mass Market Publishing Firm

The juvenile division's publisher
  and the firm's marketing director*
2 of 3 Division vice presidents*
The managing editor*
The senior editor*
The editor-art director*
1 of 2 art directors*
The firm's vp in charge of finance
The firm's trade sales directors
The juvenile production supervisor
The juvenile/adult library promotion
  and advertising director
4 of 54 trade salespeople

PATRONS OR CUSTOMERS

The Public Library

15 children's branch librarians
  interviewed plus a questionnaire
  survey of 45**
5 juvenile library coordinators
  (interviewed and given
  questionnaire)*
The library system's director

The Book Store Chain

The central book buyer*
The 4 branch store auxiliary buyers*

The Department Store Chain

The central book buyer*

*These are direct selectors; the others are indirect selectors.
**These 45 branch librarians are the only people listed on this chart who were not interviewed.

ENTERING THE ORGANIZATIONS

Some mention should be made about the manner in which entry was made into the organizations. The procedure varied depending on the organization involved. In all cases, however, the people contacted were told only in general terms that the study related to book production and distribution within the juvenile book industry. The notion of client relationships was avoided to prevent any bias in their answers; nor, for the same reason, was any mention made of a comparison between the mass market and the library market segments. A conversation on this basis with the head of the public library's juvenile division and the division's head of book selection led to a complete access to files, as well as the permission to interview 4 juvenile coordinators and 15 branch librarians (in an accidental sample of those scheduled to visit the System Coordinating Office during a certain period of time for new book ordering) and to survey all of them. In the case of the bookstore chain, the firm's central book buyer and the area's 4 branch store auxiliary buyers were contacted and interviewed. With regard to the department store, only one person coordinates juvenile book selection for all 11 branches; he was contacted and interviewed.

Interviewing the publishing firms presented the greatest complexity. In order to avoid alienating the principals of the firms with large plans to interview many people, direct and key indirect selectors were contacted and interviewed without the coordinated help of management. This approach was possible because of *Literary Marketplace,* an annual book listing the names and titles of important figures in all American publishing houses. In some cases, when a position was not listed in *Marketplace* or when selectors seemed difficult to approach individually, previously interviewed subjects were helpful in arranging a meeting. This hopscotch approach, though successful to a large degree, did have its drawbacks. One editor at the mass market firm refused to submit to an interview, and in a few cases potential interview arrangers made clear their feelings that meetings with more people in the same organizational roles were redundant and would take too much valuable time from the juvenile department as a whole. Consequently, only 1 of 3 readers and 2 of 4 associate editors were interviewed in the library market firm, and only a number of salespeople could be interviewed in both publishing houses.

Prominent figures within the children's book complex or individuals in the areas of the complex, such as book wholesaling or jobbing, about which more knowledge was desired, were contacted directly. In most cases, the same questions that were posed to the production and outlet selectors were asked of them. In a few cases, however, the discussion of broad issues, problems, and hypotheses that were being grappled with by the researcher was thought to be more useful.

THE INTERVIEWS

Essentially the same interview questions were asked of all selectors. Since the focal library system has two stages of book selection, some of the questions had to be asked twice.

In the first part of the interview, the selector was asked to describe his or her objectives and activities. The second part dealt with questions relating to the subject's role regarding specific aspects of book selection.[1] The subject was asked to note his or her degree of influence in the organization regarding each aspect of book selection, the importance of that aspect, guidelines held with respect to it, and the reasons for those guidelines. Specific probes of the influence on the selector that emerged from that question were used to explore why those influences are important and how their requirements are discovered. A question regarding controversial issues and one regarding the selector's image of the audience, and the way the image is arrived at, further illuminated specifications of selection and influences.

The third part of the interview schedule examined the selector's activities and perspectives with respect to the opposing organizations in the client relationship (the distribution outlets for the publishing selectors, the publishers for the outlet selectors). Both the publishing and outlet selectors were asked if there were any types of books that they feel outlet selectors want but that are not being published. Similarly, selectors from both types of organizations were asked about the extent and nature of their contacts with representatives from the opposite organizational type. Here the intention was to gauge the manner in which the selectors either are influenced by, or attempt to influence, selectors on the other side of the client relationship. Specific probes also queried the mass market and the library market outlet selectors about the desirability of books from Global Publishing and R&A Publishing; selectors from those firms, in turn, were asked about the importance of those outlets for their books. The final part of the interview schedule was comprised of questions designed to explore the respondent's professional background and previous experience in the industry.

The open-ended nature of the questions allowed the interviewer to clarify and pursue in some depth interesting comments by the respondent. Most interviews ranged from 45 minutes to an hour, though several were longer and some were shorter. Direct selectors usually had longer interviews than indirect selectors; interviews with librarians were the longest of all. Some interview subjects were more open than others, though none was diffident or unresponsive. Naturally, selectors dwelled on some areas of the interview schedule more than others, depending on their areas of professional responsibility. For example, the publishing firms' marketing and sales people spent most of their time on parts 1 and 3, while the editors and librarians were more talkative on 1 and 2.

In many of the interviews with direct selectors a tape recorder was used and the results transcribed. When a tape recorder was not present, quick notes were taken and fleshed out immediately after the meeting.

123

Analysis of the interviews was performed through grouping the responses by organization and segment and by comparing the answers of the selectors to each question. Piecing together the various repondents' comments in part 1 about their own and others' responsibilities and duties yielded pictures of each organization's structure and children's book selection process. The respondents' specifications regarding the aspects of book selection in part 2 were listed and compared, as were the influences they said brought about those specifications.

The answers in part 3 were similarly sifted and analyzed with the aim of clarifying some of the more formal mechanisms by which organizations interacting in a client relationship attempt to learn about and influence each other. The background data in part 4 was used to compare the professional experience of selectors in each segment and to determine the extent to which the two segments exchange personnel. Through synthesizing the interview responses in this manner and comparing the findings in each segment, a picture of the major client relationship's influence upon the structure and process of content selection in each organization was obtained.

Response Bias

A concern in any study based to a large extent on interviews is the degree to which there exists a pattern of bias that makes suspect any relationship between the answers given and the respondents' actual activities. It is probably impossible to prevent self-aggrandizing talk on the part of interview subjects. However, with a firm promise to the respondents that personal and organizational anonymity was assured, an attempt was made to minimize pressures conducive to outright prevarication.

It should also be noted that the answers collected in the five organizations did not yield a simple consistency that would imply publicity-oriented responses. Rather, the varied responses revealed activities from different points of view that could be seen to converge, yielding a mosaic of the children's book industry that could be analyzed in a systematic fashion. This convergence of responses, plus the consistency with which responses did match certain findings about the actual books produced and distributed in each segment, lends a strong confidence in the validity of the research.

THE QUESTIONNAIRE SURVEY

It was noted above that a decision was made to interview a one-third sample of the 45 branch librarians plus the four coordinators, with the distribution of a survey questionnaire to the entire population afterward. The questionnaire was designed to test certain hypotheses that had been formulated about the library book selection process as a result of the interviews. Completed by 35 librarians, the questionnaire was similar in thrust to the interview schedule. In the first part the respondents were presented with a list of 40 particular influences that were mentioned as important in the interviews and were asked whether each influence was very important, somewhat important, or not important at all in their thinking regarding the selection of books. The second part queried respondents about the importance of those influences for them in their branches.[2] The third part presented questions regarding a selector's activities and perspectives with respect to the opposing organizations in the client relationship. The final part asked for information about the librarians' branch and professional background.

The questionnaire responses were totaled by computer. As in the case of the interviews, answers by coordinators and branch librarians were grouped separately and compared. The survey results and the interview results were compared on similar issues. Conclusions from that analysis were supplemented with impressions from nonparticipant observations of library selection activities, as well as with information from formal library documents about book choosing procedures.

Notes

Introduction

1. George Gerbner, "Institutional Pressurers on Mass Communicators," *Sociological Review Monograph* no. 13 (1969), p. 243.

2. Selma Lanes, *Down the Rabbit Hole: Adventures and Misadventures in the Realm of Children's Literature* (New York: Stein and Day, 1970), pp. 113–14.

3. See, for example, Warren Breed, "Social Control in the Newsroom: A Functional Analysis," *Social Forces* 33: 326–35 (1955); Muriel Cantor, *The Hollywood TV Producer: His Work and His Audience* (New York: Basic Books, 1971); Edward Jay Epstein, *News from Nowhere* (New York: Vintage Books, 1973); Walter Gieber, "News Is What Newspapermen Make It," in Lewis Dexter and David White, eds., *People, Society, and Mass Communications* (New York: Free Press, 1959), pp. 173–82; Lee Sigelman, "Reporting the News," *American Journal of Sociology* 79, 1: 132–51 (July 1973); Gaye Tuchman, "Objectivity as Strategic Ritual: An Examination of Newsmen's Notions of Objectivity," *American Journal of Sociology* 77, 4: 600–70 (January 1972); and David M. White, "The Gatekeeper: A Case Study in the Selection of News," *Journalism Quarterly* 27, 4: 383–90 (Fall 1950).

4. As interesting examples, see Hortense Powdermaker, *Hollywood: The Dream Factory* (New York: Little, Brown, 1951); and Serge Denisoff, *Solid Gold: The Popular Music Industry* (New Brunswick, N.J.: Transaction Books, 1975).

5. Paul Hirsch, "Processing Fads and Fashions: An Organization-Set Analysis of Cultural Industry Systems," *American Journal of Sociology* 77: 639–59 (1972).

6. Gerbner, "Institutional Pressures on Mass Communicators."

7. It is clear that one important difference between the library market and the mass market is that while in the former books are borrowed by the ultimate readers, in the latter books are bought. This difference will be seen to have some consequence for the production of titles in both segments. It is important to emphasize, however, that the focus of the present investigation is not on the buying or borrowing habits of consumers but, rather, on the forces that influence the spectrum of books which are made available for lending or selling.

8. *Publishers Weekly* (16 June 1975), pp. 3–30.

9. *School Library Journal* (16 January 1975), p. 109.

10. Henry Drennan and Doris Holladay, *Statistics of Public Libraries, Part I* (Washington, D.C.: U.S. Department of Health, Education, and Welfare, 1962), p. 4.

11. Herbert S. Bailey, Jr. *The Art and Science of Book Publishing* (New York: Harper and Row, 1970); John Dessauer, *Book Publishing: What It Is, What It Does* (New York: R. R. Bowker, 1974); Chandler Grannis, ed., *What Happens in Book Publishing* (New York: Columbia University Press, 1967); Jean Spealman Kujoth, ed., *Book Publishing: Inside Views* (Metuchen, N.J.: Scarecrow Press, 1971); *The Author and His Audience* (Philadelphia: J. B. Lippincott, 1967); and Datus Smith, *A Guide to Book Publishing* (New York: R. R. Bowker, 1966).

12. Jean Karl, "The Children's Book Department," in Chandler Grannis, ed., *What Happens in Book Publishing.*

13. Lanes, *Down the Rabbit Hole*, pp. 114–29.

14. Lewis Coser, "Publishers as Gatekeepers of Ideas," *The Annals* 421:22 (September 1975).

15. William Jenkins, "The Future of Children's Books," in Kujoth, ed., *Book Publishing: Inside Views.*

16. John Rowe Townsend, *A Sense of Story* (New York: Longman's, 1971) and *Written for Children: An Outline of English Children's Literature* (New York: Lothrop, 1967).

17. See, for example, Elinor Whitney Field, compiler, *Horn Book Reflections: on Children's Books and Reading* (Boston: Horn Book, 1969).

18. Lenore J. Weitzman; Deborah Eifler; Elizabeth Hokado; and Catherine Ross, "Sex-Role Socialization in Picture Books for Pre-School Children," *American Journal of Sociology* 77, 6: 1125–50 (May, 1972).

19. See, for example, Dorothy M. Broderick, *An Introduction to Children's Work in Public Libraries* (New York: H. W. Wilson Company, 1965); and Elizabeth H. Gross, *Public Library Service to Children* (Dobbs Ferry, N.Y.: Oceana Publications, 1967).

2. May Hill Arbuthnot and Zena Sutherland, *Children and Books*, 4th ed. (Glenview, Ill.: Scott, Foresman and Company, 1972); Paul Hazard, *Books, Children, and Men*, trans. by Marguerite Mitchell, 4th ed. (Boston: Horn Book, 1960); Jean Karl, *From Childhood to Childhood: Children's Books and Their Creators* (New York: Stein and Day, 1970); and Cornelia Meigs, Anne Eaton, Elizabeth Nesbitt, and Ruth Viguers, *A Critical History of Children's Literature*, rev. ed. (New York: Macmillan, 1969).

21. Gross, *Public Library Service to Children*, p. 21.

22. Examples are Dorothy M. Broderick, " 'Problem' Nonfiction," *Library Journal* 87: 3378 (1 October 1962); Charles Busha, *The Attitudes of Midwestern Public Librarians Toward Intellectual Freedom and Censorship* (Ph.D. diss., Indiana University, 1971); May Linda Eakin, *Censorship in Public High School Libraries* (M.A. thesis, Columbia University, 1948); Marjorie Fiske, *Book Selection and Censorship* (Berkeley: University of California Press, 1959); Eric Moon, " 'Problem' Fiction," *Library Journal* 87: 484–96 (1 January 1962); Michael Pope, *Sex and the Undecided Librarian: A Study of Librarians' Opinions*

on Sexually Oriented Literature (Metuchen, N.J.: Scarecrow Press, 1974); and Eldon W. Tamblyn, "They Play It Safe," *Library Journal* 90: 2495–98 (1 June 1965).

23. *The Bowker Annual of Library and Book Trade Information* (New York: R. R. Bowker, 1977), pp. 271–77. The public library was chosen over the city's school library system because of the important national, regional, and local significance it has, an influence that extends to its school-based counterpart.

Chapter 1

1. Cornelia Meigs, Anne Eaton, Elizabeth Nesbitt, and Ruth Viguers, *A Critical History of Children's Literature*, rev. ed. (New York: Macmillan, 1969), p. 384.

2. See Harriet Long, *Public Library Service to Children: Foundation and Development* (Metuchen, N.J.: Scarecrow Press, 1969), p. 84. Also see John Tebbel, *A History of the American Book Publishing Industry*, vol. 2 (New York: R. R. Bowker, 1974), p. 519.

3. Long, p. 48.

4. Ibid., p. 48.

5. Ibid., p. 49.

6. Tebbel, p. 597.

7. Long, p. 85.

8. Meigs, et al., p. 386.

9. Ibid., p. 388.

10. Tebbel, p. 601.

11. *The Horn Book* (August 1928), pp. 74–76.

12. *The Horn Book* (October 1974), pp. 84–87.

13. Meigs, et al., p. 410.

14. *The Bowker Catalog, 1977–1978* (New York: R. R. Bowker, 1978), p. 42.

Chapter 3

1. Sara Innis Fenwick, "Library Service to Children and Young People," *Library Trends* 25: 329 (July, 1976).

2. It might be noted that while a full 80% (28) of the 35 questionnaire respondents said that parents generally help children ages 3–5 choose books and 60% (21) said the same is true for children 6–8, only 2 respondents considered parents an important additional factor to think about separately from the child, except in cases of complaint (which were not characterized as frequent). Perhaps the librarians' ignoring of parents as separate considerations in book selection can be explained by that fact that 43% (15) of the surveyed librarians felt parents know very little about what their children really like while

another 29% (10) felt they know something, but not much about the subject. It is interesting to note that the 10 librarians who said parents know a lot were from areas where the children have excellent reading abilities and where, according to the two interviewed subjects, parents watch their children's reading habits —and librarians' buying habits— closely.

3. The reader will note that extra-library and extra-divisional bodies (PTAs, the city and state governments, the library director and trustees) have not been noted as structuring the librarians' perceptions of general requirements. This omission is in accordance with the failure of any respondent to mention them, except with regard to the routine doling of funds, and in line with the fact that they were among the factors considered not important by over 70% of the survey respondents. It should be pointed out, however, that these answers do not reflect the implicit, encompassing influences of the above-mentioned entities as Metrosystem's key patrons (the city and state governments), as the pressure groups that impinge upon the patrons (PTAs and others), or as Metrosystem's managerial links between its patrons and its operations (the director and the trustees).

In other words, it may be speculated that if these and other key establishment figures became vocally displeased with Metrosystem's approach to book selection, their displeasure would, at the very least, be taken as an invitation to a serious reexamination and perhaps revamping of the entire process. The library director did note when interviewed, however, that the reputation and expertise of the head of book selection has led him to devolve virtual autonomy in selection matters upon her. And, since there has not been a critical incident in the recent past in which an extraorganizational factor has significantly challenged the boundaries of the division's public interest stance, the librarians have had no cause to consider patrons or pressure groups when reviewing and choosing books.

4. The fact that the librarians can select books they want to review means (as many noted) that they often choose titles by authors they like. This situation would seem to strengthen the chances of acceptability of library market personalities and, also, perpetuate the strength of certain firms in that market.

5. It is evident that not all the books which were received by the division during this period were published during fall, 1974 and spring, 1975. However, the time frames do overlap closely enough to make the findings comparable.

Chapter 4

1. John Tebbel, *A History of the American Book Publishing Industry,* vol. 2 (New York: R. R. Bowker, 1974), pp. 481–88.

2. Ibid., pp. 365, 498.

3. Cornelia Meigs, Anne Eaton, Elizabeth Nesbitt, and Ruth Viguers, *A Critical History of Children's Literature,* rev. ed. (New York: Macmillan, 1969), p. 402.

4. Unfortunately, very little has been written on this aspect of publishing history. Tebbel (p. 293) notes that "In the 1930s, Rand McNally was the first publisher to go into the mass production and distribution of children's books, introducing quality [sic] into such lines, to be sold in chain stores at prices from fifteen to twenty five cents." The rest of the information in these paragraphs has been obtained through interviews with principals at Western Publishing and Rand McNally.

5. As Golden Books grew in popularity and price, this policy was changed so that only the more expensive Golden titles are returnable—and only partially so.

Chapter 5

1. One structural difference may be suggested at this point as traceable to the client relationship: while all the 9 direct selectors in the R&A are women, 5 of the 9 Global direct selectors, including the section heads and publisher, are men. Although no general cross-segment comparisons are available on this issue, it is tempting to suggest that the observed editorial domination by women in library market publishing firms seems to have been sustained, at least in part, by the fact that the library population with whom they interact is overwhelmingly female. This situation does not seem to be true in the mass market. Buyers for stores do not seem to be predominantly female. Moreover, mass market editors, unlike their library market counterparts, have very little contact with outlet selectors.

2. The reason for the inability of Global to compete with the other mass market firms' discount rates is related to its philosophy of selling through popular names. While Western and Rand McNally pay a flat fee outright to creators of books that retail at under $1 and give extremely low royalties (less than 5% of wholesale price sales for their more expensive titles), Global has paid the name author-illustrators of its picture books trade book royalties (10% and more), to the point where royalty charges can encompass 25% of a book's unit cost. Under such conditions, the traditional trade jobber discount of about 48% is the highest the firm can offer to wholesalers, while other mass market firms (some of which, unlike Global, also have their own printing presses to lower costs) offer 51%, plus 10% if a certain number of units are bought. Trade jobbers buy from Global because they are geared to operate at the 48% discount level and because of the division's proven success in the outlets that they serve. IDs, however, feel they cannot make a profit with the discount which Global offers and refuse to carry its lines no matter what their potential popularity.

3. It might be noted here that the interviewed subjects uniformly assumed that parents with or without their children were the usual ultimate customers for their books. They stated, however, that no research has been carried out to verify this assumption; the managing editor characterized it as "an accepted piece of parlor wisdom."

4. The price competition in both the library and mass markets often forces decision makers who feel a book will be most successful only if sold at a particular price to set that price, even though it will not return their production costs in the first printing. The hope is that its popularity will necessitate more printings, allowing the firm to recoup costs and desired profits over a slightly longer term. It will be noted that because of the more limited nature of R&A's market (in that books are circulated, not sold) and the larger number of competing books and firms (in that Global's salespeople, who compete with only a handful of juvenile publishers, can often decide which of their division's titles should be racked against the particular books or lines of particular rivals), the library market firm cannot project as large sales for as long a time as its mass market counterparts. The price differentials of the two markets compensate for this difference, however.

5. She is called "managing editor" because she also has the chore of coordinating certain production and publicity activities within the department.

6. At the time this study was conducted, the editor of the "easy readers" section had resigned and the editor-in-chief had taken his place. This move, which made the editor-in-chief head of two sections, was expected to be temporary.

7. In the production of "unattached" titles, sectional jurisdiction might not be observed. For example, the editor-in-chief usually edits the unattached picture books by the firm's name talent, and the novelty books editor has edited a large-format activity book. It might also be noted that the vice president of the novelty books section is the liaison with the two book clubs and in charge of developing the division's own mail order apparatus based on the small, lightweight paperback picturebooks.

Chapter 6

1. Interestingly, Global does offer some juvenile cooperative advertising money to outlets, but it is rarely used.

Chapter 7

1. Gaye Tuchman, "Making News By Doing Work: Routinizing the Unexpected," *American Journal of Sociology* 79: 119–31 (July, 1971); and John March and Herbert Simon, *Organizations* (New York: John Wiley, 1958).

2. Arthur Stinchcombe, "Bureaucratic and Craft Administration of Production," *Administrative Science Quarterly* 4: 168–87 (1958). Quotes are from pages 170 and 171.

3. See Denis McQuail, "Uncertainty about the Audience and the Organization of Mass Communications," *Sociological Review Monograph* no. 13 (1969), pp. 75–84, for a review of this area. McQuail's suggestions about the conse-

quences that a lack of information about the audience has for the approach of British Broadcasting Corporation selectors to their work parallel some of the findings of the present study. However, he attributes those attitudes simply to the difficulties confronted by members of a mass media organization in knowing their audience. Because he reifies the concept, he does not consider that the implicit audience images which are revealed in the BBC approach to programming might reflect objectives that have evolved through and are reinforced by intra- and extra-organizational considerations. Nor, for the same reason, does he predict that any audience selectors might try to ascertain would probably also reflect those objectives.

4. William Melody, *Children's Television: The Economics of Exploitation* (New Haven: Yale University Press, 1973).

5. See "Research on Television and the Young," a series of articles in the *Journal of Communication* 26: 95–171 (Spring, 1976).

6. Melody, p. 138.

7. The "prime time access rule," instituted in 1970 and varied somewhat since then, currently says that in the top fifty television markets where three or more commercial television stations operate, networks may not program their affiliates for more than three hours in the prime time segment, 7:00–11:00 PM (Eastern time), six days a week. Anticipating affiliates would fill this time with off-network or feature film reruns, the FCC prohibited such shows. The rule, it was hoped, would create a market for new package-produced, or syndicated programs.

8. See *Publishers Weekly* (February 24, 1975), p. 63.

9. Elizabeth Gross, *Public Library Service to Children* (Dobbs Ferry, N.Y.: Oceana Publications, 1967), p. 21.

Appendix

1. Those aspects were: The size of the selection list; the relative selection of fiction and nonfiction titles; the relative selection of fantasy and reality titles; the relative selection of books for general audiences vs. titles for particular ethnic and/or racial groups; the relative selection of books for different ages and/or grades; the author and illustrator; the subject of the book; the plot; the illustrations; the characters and the way they are portrayed (probe on racial mix, animals vs. people, sexual mix); the moral point of view; the style (probe on poetry vs. prose, first or third person narration, vocabulary difficulty control); the accuracy; the size of the book (probe on dimensions, length); the binding of the book; the overall design (probe on typography, margin sizes, frontispiece design, quality of paper); the price; the paperback format.

2. The influences were: The total book buying budget of the Children's Division; the branch's book-buying budget; the opinions of coordinators who read the book; the *Kirkus* review of the book; reviews of the book in professional review media other than *Kirkus;* opinion of the librarian who wrote the system-

level review of the book (applies to branch-selection only); the reputation of the author; the reputation of the illustrator; the reputation of the book publisher; the chief coordinator; the head of book selection; personal likes and dislikes; branch's current circulation figures; philosophy about what children ought to read; general impressions about what the city's children like to read; general impressions about what children who come to the branch like to read; ethnic and racial minorities from around the city; ethnic and racial minorities from the branch area; older children who are slow readers; advanced readers; the potential popularity of the book in terms of circulation; the extent to which the book is of very high quality; the size of the month's selection list; the cost of the book; the extent to which the book will balance the collection; the moral point of view in the book; the library's trustees or directors; library science students who borrow books; parents who borrow books; teachers who borrow books; school assignments given to students; the potential use of the book in a book talk; the use of the book in a book fair; potential complaints from parents; people or pressures from city or state government; publishers' book fairs; training in library school; promotional material from the publisher.

Bibliography

Arbuthnot, May Hill, and Sutherland, Zena. *Children and Books*. 4th ed. Glenview, Ill.: Scott, Foresman and Company, 1972.

The Author and His Audience. Philadelphia: J. B. Lippincott, 1967.

Bailey, Jr., Herbert S. *The Art and Science of Book Publishing*. New York: Harper and Row, 1970.

The Bowker Annual of Library and Book Trade Information. New York: R. R. Bowker, 1977.

The Bowker Catalogue 1977–1978. New York: R. R. Bowker, 1978.

Breed, Warren. "Social Control in the Newsroom: A Functional Analysis." *Social Forces* 33: 326–35 (1955).

Broderick, Dorothy M. *An Introduction to Children's Work in Public Libraries*. New York: H. W. Wilson, 1965.

——————. " 'Problem' Nonfiction." *Library Journal* 87: 3373–78 (October 1, 1962).

Busha, Charles. *The Attitudes of Midwestern Public Librarians toward Intellectual Freedom and Censorship*. Ph.D. dissertation, Indiana University, 1971.

Cantor, Muriel. *The Hollywood TV Producer: His Work and His Audience*. New York: Basic Books, 1971.

Colby, Jean. *Writing, Illustrating, and Editing Children's Books*. New York: Hastings House, 1967.

Coser, Lewis. "Publishers as Gatekeepers of Ideas." *The Annals* 421: 14–22 (September, 1975).

Denisoff, R. Serge. *Solid Gold: The Popular Music Industry*. New Brunswick, N.J.: Transaction Books, 1975.

Dessauer, John. *Book Publishing: What It Is, What It Does*. New York: R. R. Bowker, 1974.

Drennan, Henry, and Holladay, Doris. *Statistics of Public Libraries*, Pt. 1 Washington, D.C.: U.S. Department of Health, Education, and Welfare, 1962.

Eakin, May Lida. *Censorship in Public High School Libraries*. M.A. thesis, Columbia University, 1948.

Epstein, Edward Jay. *News from Nowhere*. New York: Vintage Books, 1973.

Fenwick, Sara Innis. "Library Service to Children and Young People." *Library Trends* 25: 329–50. (July, 1976).

Field, Elinor Whitney, compiler. *Horn Book Reflections: On Children's Books and Reading.* Boston: The Horn Book, 1969.

Fiske, Marjorie. *Book Selection and Censorship.* Berkeley: University of California Press, 1969.

Gerbner, George. "Institutional Pressures on Mass Communicators." *Sociological Review Monographs* no. 13 (1969), pp. 205–48.

————. "Communication and Social Environment." *Scientific American* 227.3: 153–60 (September, 1972).

Gerhardt, Lillian, compiler. *Issues in Children's Book Selection.* New York: R. R. Bowker, 1974.

Gieber, Walter. "News Is What Newspapermen Make It." *People, Society, and Mass Communications.* Edited by Lewis Dexter and David White. New York: Free Press, 1959.

Gross, Elizabeth H. *Public Library Service to Children.* Dobbs Ferry, N.Y.: Oceana Publications, Inc., 1967.

Grannis, Chandler B. *What Happens in Book Publishing.* New York: Columbia University Press, 1967.

Guback, Thomas H. "Film as International Business." *Journal of Communication* 24, 1: 90–102 (Winter, 1974).

Hazard, Paul. *Books, Children, and Men.* 4th ed. Translated by Marguerite Mitchell. Boston: *The Horn Book,* 1960.

Hirsch, Paul. "Processing Fads and Fashions: An Organization-Set Analysis of Cultural Industry Systems." *American Journal of Sociology* 77: 639–59 (1972).

Jenkins, William A. "The Future of Children's Books." *Book Publishing: Inside Views.* Edited by Jean S. Kujoth. Metuchen, N.J.: Scarecrow Press, 1971.

Karl, Jean. *From Childhood to Childhood: Children's Books and Their Creators.* New York: Stein and Day, 1970.

————. "The Children's Book Department." In *What Happens in Book Publishing.* Edited by Chandler B. Grannis. New York: Columbia University Press, 1967.

Kujoth, Jean Spealman, editor. *Book Publishing: Inside Views.* Metuchen, N.J.: Scarecrow Press, 1971.

Lanes, Selma G. *Down the Rabbit Hole: Adventures and Misadventures in the Realm of Children's Literature.* New York: Atheneum, 1971.

Long, Harriet. *Public Library Service to Children: Foundation and Development.* Metuchen, N.J.: Scarecrow Press, 1969.

McQuail, Denis. "Uncertainty about the Audience and the Organization of Mass Communications." *Sociological Review Monographs* no. 13 (1969), pp. 75–84.

March, James, and Simon, Herbert. *Organizations.* New York: John Wiley, 1958.

Meigs, Cornelia; Eaton, Anne; Nesbitt, Elizabeth; and Viguers, Ruth. *A Critical History of Children's Literature.* Rev. ed. New York: Macmillan, 1969.

Melody, William. *Children's TV: The Economics of Exploitation.* New Haven: Yale University Press, 1973.

Moon, Eric. " 'Problem' Fiction." *Library Journal* 87: 484–96 (January 1, 1962).

Pope, Michael. *Sex and the Undecided Librarian: A Study of Librarians' Opinions on Sexually Oriented Literature.* Metuchen, N.J.: Scarecrow Press, 1974.

Powdermaker, Hortense. *Hollywood: The Dream Factory.* Boston: Little, Brown, 1951.

Sigelman, Lee. "Reporting the News." *American Journal of Sociology* 79, 1: 132–51 (July, 1973).

Smith, Datus C. *A Guide to Book Publishing.* New York: R. R. Bowker, 1966.

Stinchcombe, Arthur. "Bureaucratic and Craft Administration of Production." *Administrative Science Quarterly* 4: 168–87 (1958).

Tamblyn, Eldon W. "They Play It Safe." *Library Journal* 90: 2495–98 (June 1, 1965).

Tebbel, John. *A History of the American Book Publishing Industry.* Vol. 2. New York: R. R. Bowker, 1974.

Townsend, John R. *A Sense of Story.* New York: Longman's 1971.

——————. *Written for Children: An Outline of English Children's Literature.* New York: Lothop, 1967.

Tuchman, Gaye. "Objectivity as Strategic Ritual: An Examination of Newsmen's Notions of Objectivity." *American Journal of Sociology* 77, 4: 600–79 (January, 1972).

——————. "Making News by Doing Work: Routinizing the Unexpected." *American Journal of Sociology* 79: 110–31 (July, 1971).

Weitzman, Lenore J.; Eifler, Deborah; Hokado, Elizabeth; and Ross, Catherine. "Sex-Role Socialization in Picture Books for Preschool Children." *American Journal of Sociology* 77, 6: 1125–50 (May, 1972).

White, David M. " 'Gatekeeper': A Case Study in the Selection of News." *Journalism Quarterly* 27, 4: 383–90 (Fall, 1950).

Wright, Charles R. *Mass Communication: A Sociological Perspective.* 2d ed. New York: Random House, 1975.